COMMON WORSHIP YEAR B

DIY Guide to All-age Worship

12 services for special occasions

Tim Storey

kevin
mayhew

First published in 2002 by
KEVIN MAYHEW LTD
Buxhall, Stowmarket, Suffolk, IP14 3BW
Email: info@kevinmayhewltd.com

© 2002 Tim Storey

The right of Tim Storey to be identified as the author
of this work has been asserted by him in accordance
with the Copyright, Designs and Patents Act, 1988.

The OHP sheets and scorecards may be photocopied
without copyright infringement provided they are
used for the purpose for which they are intended.
Reproduction of any of the contents of this book
for commercial purposes is subject to the usual
copyright restrictions.

No other part of this publication may be reproduced, stored in a
retrieval system, or transmitted, in any form or by any means,
electronic, mechanical, photocopying, recording or otherwise,
without the prior written permission of the publisher.

All rights reserved.

9 8 7 6 5 4 3 2 1 0

ISBN 1 84003 985 X
Catalogue No. 1500545

Cover design by Angela Selfe
Edited and typeset by Elisabeth Bates

Printed and bound in Great Britain

Contents

Introduction			5
Who, when and how long			9
What to put in and what to leave out			11
The four key people			15
How you can begin			19
The Services and how to use them			21
Advent Sunday	Look out!	*Luke 21:25-36*	23
Christmas Day	Unwrapping Christmas	*Luke 2:1-14*	27
New Year	God is in charge	*Psalm 148*	31
Epiphany	The Light shines in the darkness	*Matthew 2:1-12*	37
Lent	Oops – I did it again	*Matthew 4:1-11*	45
Mother's Day	Mary – a VSM (Very Special Mum)!	*Luke 2:33-35*	51
Good Friday	Making the cut	*John 19:1-27*	57
Easter Sunday	Surprise, surprise!	*John 20:1-18*	67
Ascension	Gone but not forgotten	*Acts 1:1-11*	73
Pentecost	Fruit, lovely fruit!	*Acts 2:1-21*	79
Trinity Sunday	Three into One WILL go	*John 3:1-17*	85
Harvest	Looking after God's world	*Genesis 1:1-13*	91

Introduction

Few churches go through a month without having at least one service that is described as 'Family' or 'All-age' Worship and some churches are fortunate enough to have gifted leaders and speakers who not only make the service exciting for the younger members of the congregation but also meaningful for older members. Even churches with such people would admit that there is a great difficulty in keeping the material fresh and not submitting to the temptation to keep pushing the barriers of worship to the point that it becomes entertainment rather than worship. The job is even harder for those churches without people gifted in these areas. This book is aimed at encouraging and further equipping those who are already actively involved in All-age Worship and enabling those who aren't but would like to be or who are struggling to explore the possibilities of All-age Worship with some simple, yet practical, advice as to how to improve what is there . . . or even start with a fresh new service.

The point

I remember someone telling me that he had returned to a school he had previously visited and was greeted enthusiastically by a child with the words, 'I remember you – you came here before and stood on your head and ate a daffodil! But I can't, for the life of me, remember why!' The greatest danger of any work with children is that the 'service', whether it be a school assembly or in a church on Sunday, becomes so focused on keeping the children's attention that they are not required to think about what is going on – and thereby miss the point of the exercise. This is not to say that we should not aim to make our services exciting! It is to say that they must be exciting, radical, fun and visual but, most of all, they must be relevant.

Celia Morris, from the Frontline Church in Liverpool, recommends this principle when working with children:

- What is the one thing you want them to take away?
- What is the one issue you want to challenge them about?
- What is the one thing you want them to apply in their lives?

This applies equally to All-age/Family Worship. Before any service begins to be planned, there needs to be a clear understanding of the basic point of the exercise. It doesn't need to be complicated: 'God loves you' is a vital piece of knowledge that needs to be understood in both the head and the heart of every child – and far more important than trying to convey the differences between pre-millennialism and post-millennialism!

All age?

The reality of All-age or Family Worship in the twenty-first century is that neither title truly satisfies what we are trying to do in the services we are talking about. I remember the 'Family Services' of my childhood and recall that they were very little different from the other services – except that the speaker did some things for the children.

Some churches sadly still believe that 'Family' worship means a token five-minute talk for the children in the middle of an hour and a half of 'adult' worship. It is hard enough to keep children interested when the whole service revolves around them, so it is not a surprise that children as well as some adults (on the whole) struggle with such 'Family' services.

The other problem with 'Family' services is the very title itself. What is a 'family' in the twenty-first century? We may well accept that the biblical understanding of family involves two parents (of opposite gender) but the postmodern family may be very different. Whilst we may proclaim (and truly believe) that the single parent family is as welcome and relevant as the traditional mum, dad and 2.4 kids, the fact is that many people perceive the title 'Family Service' as discriminatory. We may know that it isn't, but perception is nine-tenths of the truth and if we want such services to grow, losing the 'family' tag is a positive move. It is also worth pointing out that many biblical families consisted of husbands with quite a few wives and numerous difficulties with half-siblings – so maybe the biblical model isn't so different after all!

At the other end of the spectrum is the Toddler Service, where everything is pitched at the youngest age group. This can be great fun (and my study is filled with cotton-wool sheep, Zacchaeus palm trees, Christmas crowns and other such memorabilia) but whilst this caters for that age group, it can only ever have limited use for the older age range (of both children and adults). Toddler Services are, as a stand-alone midweek session, fantastic opportunities for outreach but not a good model for a Sunday 'All-age' service.

Indeed, the title 'All-age' Worship presents problems in itself. Does it mean that you pitch the service at one level and hope that all can relate to it – the *bullet* approach? Or does it mean that the service contains a variety of layers that are aimed at different age groups – the *shotgun* approach? Both have advantages and both present problems: I believe the answer is somewhere between the two.

I aim most all-age worship at the 7-year-olds and talk in language that they can understand, avoiding jargon wherever possible and explaining things in ways I hope they can appreciate – the bullet approach. Equally, within that language and approach, I aim to provide thoughts that will stimulate discussion and further thought in the adults present and will, for example, say 'Now, here's a thought for the adults . . .' – the shotgun approach. One thing to be made clear is that pitching all age worship at 7-year-olds does not mean banal and thin worship: the average 7-year-old is able to cope with concepts and a world view far beyond the 7-year-old of previous generations: he or she is computer-literate and aware of news, sexual politics and a vast array of issues. Those below the age of 7 may not have the breadth of understanding, but they will pick up on a lot more than we may give them credit for and will be stimulated by anything visual. Those over the age of 7 will realise that this is beneath them but will, I believe, be surprisingly engaging, so long as you engage with them! Teenagers . . . ah, teenagers! How do we engage them in all-age worship? Simply involve them: get them reading, praying, playing, making coffee . . . whatever!

This may seem a simplified approach, but it should be seen only as a principle to be applied. For example, what if you have no 7-year-olds, or every one of your children is under 5 or over 10? The answer is 'apply it': make sure the under-5s have an activity to keep them occupied whilst you spend ten minutes providing something more attuned to the adults – or aim the service at the 12-year-olds, and thereby need very little for the adults as they will probably not keep up with the 12-year-olds!

One important facet of the changing culture in which we live and work is that children today now engage far more with a visual (as opposed to a written) culture. All-age Worship inevitably features concepts and children now work far more in conceptualised thinking rather than the lateral thinking of former generations. All-age Worship needs to be couched in conceptual thinking – in other words, the 'one' statements mentioned earlier evolve into the 'one concept we are exploring today is . . .' Illustrating a concept requires more than just words – pictures, things to touch, moving around the church, etc.

Visually, the word 'clarity' is important. Overheads need to be crisp and clear with text in a reasonable size (22pt is a good size to aim for). Don't forget that some children (and some adults) will be unable to read and so it is a good idea to use repetition or short phrases.

The best suggestion to deal with the titles of 'Family' or 'All Age' is to lose them completely! Find a natty title that works for you, whether it be 'Not the Supermarket Hour on Sunday' or 'Bible Bungee Jumping' . . . be creative and inventive!

Common Worship and all that . . .

The Church of England introduced a new prayer book at the end of 2000 called *Common Worship* and the service plans in this book are based on Year B in the cycle of readings that *Common Worship* uses. The structure of services themselves is based around the 'Service of the Word', a highly flexible service contained in *Common Worship* that provides a balance of elements within all services, including those aimed at all ages:

- A **Clear Beginning**
- A **Prayer of Repentance** (Confession)
- A **Prayer of the Assurance of Forgiveness** (Absolution)
- Expressions of **Worship** spoken or sung
- A **Reading from the Bible**
- Some form of **Teaching**
- **Prayers** including our requests to God (intercession)
- The **Lord's Prayer**
- A **Statement of what we believe**
- An **Ending** that draws together our thoughts

The sections that follow in this book aim to provide a 'way in' to each of these elements – to lay down principles rather than definitive ways to put on a service.

Ultimately, each service and every element or aspect of each service is determined by a combination of influences: the people taking part, the nature and age range of the congregation, the theme being covered, the events during the week preceding the service, and so on and so forth. All-age Worship based around the Service of the Word provides a framework on which a diverse group of people builds an act of worship using a combination of appropriate resources.

Each act of worship, all-age or otherwise, is an offering of our love to God, a place where we meet with him and acknowledge our need of him. It is, therefore, personal and requires us to engage with God as well as with the material we use. It is not a performance, neither is it entertainment, but if we are to worship in Spirit and Truth, then it must come from our heart, but with our head engaged!

Who, when and how long

Who does it?

The key problems with All-age Worship (we'll keep calling it this for ease!) is that it needs to have people to do it and people with the right gifts. Enthusiasm is an essential ingredient but not necessarily enough: at a church I used to attend there was an extrovert with amazing gifts that everyone thought would be ideal to speak at the All-age Services but was hopeless because they rambled on for half an hour every time.

Someone who speaks the right language

If you are talking in a group and someone mentions gigabytes, rewriters or ISPs, then you either know what they are talking about – or you don't and you instantly 'switch off' from the conversation. The Church is as prone to jargon as anyone and for children it is an instant switch-off. For fairly obvious reasons, those involved in All-age Worship need to know the importance of the words they can and cannot use. Parents are clearly good people to use because they might have some idea of the latest language invading the playground!

Extroverts are born to be involved

Use them at every opportunity! If you think they might be good at leading, then let them lead and likewise at doing the talk – but handle them carefully. Your church extrovert may do a great job, or they may need telling that they tried hard but . . . well . . . it isn't really them. If this is the case, give them something else to do: they are a tremendous asset but their very nature means that they have probably given everything in their effort and may feel very hurt if slapped down.

Introverts should not be overlooked!

The idea of All-age Worship as a carefully choreographed riot may be somewhere near the truth in some cases, but may not always be helpful in building up the congregation. However, the quieter leader needs to be complemented with a more boisterous speaker and vice-versa.

Try a variety of people

An enduring frustration for both church leaders and congregations alike is that the same people are wheeled out each month: the church leader is short of time and reverts to the safe option and the member of the congregation who would love to be involved but doesn't want to push themselves forward remains frustrated for another decade. So be creative: go through the congregational list and ask whether people would like to be involved. Oh, and don't just use teachers – they do it Monday to Friday (and other times, too) and they don't like to be pigeon-holed any more than the rest of us!

Most of all – be positive!

All-age Worship is at the sharp end of much of Sunday worship. It involves taking risks and being vulnerable and often is the object of criticism from across the church age range; from the parent who says there was nothing in that service for their child to the older person who says the children didn't speak up and they couldn't hear. Criticism is inevitable – so be positive: reassure, encourage and compliment those involved, but still take risks and dream dreams!

Timing

It is a fact that you *can* have too much of a good thing! Unfortunately, many all-age services suffer from an excess of quantity over quality and people leave with the abiding memory of the five different ways they attempted to stop their child from playing with a Gameboy rather than the single point the service was trying to make. The best all-age services last about 45 minutes, contain a mix of elements (which we shall look at in a moment), a clearly recognisable theme and refreshments at some point. There are some who say that the length of a service is irrelevant – after all, we'll be spending considerably longer praising God in heaven! If we can provide the same quality of worship in our churches and sense God's presence in the same way, then I have no problem, but it is a recognised fact that the attention span of today's young people is a fraction of that of their parent's generation. Witness sound-bite TV or the in-your-face action of the modern cartoon or computer game and you get a small understanding of the changes in communication that All-age Worship must grapple with.

There are two reasons for the 45-minute suggestion: one is that it is hard to provide punchy styles of worship for any longer than that without overload or exhaustion on the part of those putting on the service and the other is that young people do not cope well with more than that length of service. 45 minutes reflects the kind of lesson timing they experience at school and the type of time-span after which they begin to get restless. This is inevitably a generalisation, but anyone who does All-age Worship on a regular basis will recognise the increased activity in certain quarters that takes place after three-quarters of an hour!

Clearly, any service works within a set of criteria and the length of a service depends on a variety of variables, some of which (but not all) can be controlled, but the target should be to finish in 45 minutes. Unfortunately, this can be a target which is rarely (if ever) met and can become a source of frustration, so a disciplined approach and careful handling of the guilty is required.

'Of course, we would have finished in time, if only . . .

. . . the notices hadn't lasted 15 minutes

. . . it wasn't Harvest/Christmas/Easter

. . . the person doing the prayers had not decided to do them without any notes

. . . we hadn't had five songs to start with

. . . the OHP hadn't given up the ghost half-way through

. . . the person doing the talk hadn't announced that he felt God was calling him to preach a totally different message from the one he had planned to . . .'

There will always be reasons! Some, such as festivals or unforeseen technical breakdowns are justifiable, others such as a lack of forethought from those involved cannot be justified. In planning services, there are ways of trying to eliminate some of these problems (not the people!) but inevitably other unavoidable problems will creep in. Ultimately, the aim must be to create a menu of items which are timed (as far as is possible) so that the unavoidable will be seen exactly as that – unavoidable but understandable things which made the service longer than usual. This is not a problem restricted to All-age Worship, but to all aspects of worship: planning is not an optional extra but an absolute necessity.

So what are the things that go together to make up the service?

What to put in and what to leave out

Elements

Like a recipe for a good meal, an all-age service needs to have a balance in the ingredients to ensure optimum nutrition. A typical service might include the following:

A **Clear Beginning** that acknowledges through either a greeting or a prayer that we have come into God's presence to worship him. It is very easy to 'fall' into a service and for everyone (including the service leader) to suddenly realise, 'Oh, we've started already!' A clear beginning (which may not be the same as a more extensive welcome that can follow in the notices) enables everyone, of all ages, to know that now is the time to think about worship.

Expressions of Praise and Worship that are spoken or sung – usually sung! Picking the right songs is a skill that needs to be recognised. There are some wonderful worship songs around, but not all of them are accessible to children and the sung worship is such a vital ingredient that it is important to stand back and try and hear the songs as the children hear them. Songs which contain jargon such as 'washed in the blood of the lamb' or the more intimate songs of love for God may be appropriate for some services, but may have little or no meaning to children and can be an instant turn-off. In short, the language of all of the service, including the sung parts, must be accessible to children: they may not necessarily need to understand all the words, but the general tenor of the message must be something they can grasp.

Some have interpreted such thoughts as meaning that the service consists entirely of 'kiddie' choruses... please, please don't! For one thing, many such songs have good and positive lyrics – but many more do not and some are theologically dodgy! Equally, a diet of such songs is like a diet of fast food: providing short-term satisfaction but little nutrition. A broad, balanced, diet of good-quality worship songs with accessible lyrics and at least one song specifically aimed at children (preferably with actions) will be a positive starting point for any All-age Worship.

A **Prayer of Repentance** (Confession) and a **Prayer of the Assurance of Forgiveness** (Absolution), to recognise our need of God's forgiveness and acknowledge his forgiveness. The need for corporate confession is challenged in some churches but I believe it is a vital ingredient in all aspects of worship, especially in All-age Worship. In a world where (in the words of Elton John) 'Sorry seems to be the hardest word', confession is not only good for the soul, it is at the heart of the Christian message: a simple recognition that we are fallible and that failing is what took Jesus to the cross. In our faith, and in our worship too, the cross is as important as the empty tomb and neither could have happened without the other – songs of victory need to be complemented with something of what the victory was over. Whilst adults may be conscious of sin during the week and repent of it at the time, it is not only good to think about it in the 'cold light of day', it is important to teach children of the need for the awareness of their sin and the need to confess it.

The reassurance of the message of forgiveness (absolution) is equally important because without it there is a great risk of feeling that our pleas for forgiveness will have drifted into space with only a dim hope of being answered.

A **Reading from the Bible**. As usual, be creative! Many people now have access to the Bible on a computer, which allows for it to be dramatised or split into a variety of parts. If the language of the version that is in your church is hard to understand, use something else, such as *The Message* (Eugene H. Peterson, Navpress) or the *Contemporary English Version*, which are written to be read aloud. And don't be tied to the lectern: put people in the pulpit (e.g. prophets), in the balcony (e.g. angels) at the back of church or in the congregation itself (e.g. the crowd) or even use a microphone in the vestry for God!

Some form of **Teaching**, for example, a Sermon or All-age Talk, expressed as a drama or poem. **Prayers** including our requests to God (Intercession), and the **Lord's Prayer**. We'll look at these in just a moment.

A **Statement of what we believe**, as a said Creed or an appropriate song that reminds us of the eternal truths that bind us together. Again, some question the need or relevance of including this on a weekly basis, but I believe that it is important that we do this. There are few churches without some difference of opinion existing about one aspect of church life or another. Along with the **Peace** (which may play a part in Communion services) a Creed offers the opportunity to recognise that the things that bind us together are far greater than anything that divides. A simple format is vital in All-age Worship and a song such as 'I believe in Jesus' or 'Lord, I lift your name on high' may provide an alternative statement of our faith, if introduced as such. It is good, too, to explain aspects of the creed to those (of all ages) who may have said them without understanding either their meaning or implication.

An **Ending** that draws together our thoughts and encourages us to go and put the challenges and encouragements into action with a prayer for God's blessing and help to do it. In the same way we recognised the point where we came in, it is important to recognise when we are leaving!

Jesus told us in John 4:24 that 'God is spirit, and his worshippers must worship in spirit and in truth.' Despite the enormous number and variety of churches around, no one church can claim to offer perfect worship and one result of that is that we should constantly be striving to make our worship more spiritual and honest – and we need help, however good we might think we are at it!

Inevitably, there are times when our worship suffers because we accidentally 'lose' one of the elements mentioned above or we try things that are theologically inaccurate (i.e. they don't actually fit with the accepted biblical-based understanding of God). This is not to say we shouldn't experiment with different forms of worship: this is vital if the Church is going to reach new areas of the community – but even experimental worship still requires the components mentioned above in order to achieve integrity. Despite years of training and experience Church leaders, too, have an incomplete understanding of worship and need to refer with confidence to resources that have been worked through and can be trusted as theologically accurate and culturally applicable.

It is vital, therefore, that we have a balance of these elements and that we use them appropriately in worship. The key question is the mixture of ingredients. When my brother was a student, he got a summer job in the local cake factory and managed to bring the whole factory to a standstill when a lack of concentration (probably involving a young lady) led him to read 'pounds' instead of 'ounces' in the pink colouring for the cake mixture. His face was as pink as the clothes he came home in! Having the right ingredients is one thing – ensuring the right quantity of each is another. Most of the items on the list above are self-explanatory but there are two which are notoriously liable to go over the allotted time (the **talk** and the **intercessions**) and something else which isn't mentioned (the **notices**).

The first two of these can usually be allocated a strict time limit but notices have a nasty habit of running away with time and it is incredibly easy for a service leader to overlook this. It is vital to know what notices are needed, prioritise and (if needs be) leave unnecessary ones out (even though the person who gave them to you will tell you that they are matters of life or death!). Keep them short and snappy and display the key points using an OHP before and after the service. Notices are a big enough turn off for adults – imagine the yawn factor for a 7-year-old!

The four key people

There are four people involved in any all-age service who jointly hold the key as to its success. To varying degrees, the amount and the way they communicate determine how successfully the aims of the service are achieved. They are...

(i) The service leader

Ultimately, someone has to 'own' the vision of the service: they need to have a clear understanding of the overall 'point' of the service, mentioned at the beginning of the introduction. This is the job of the service leader and they have a responsibility to communicate with all the people involved in the service including the other three key people, as well as everyone else: those reading, those bringing forward the collection, those doing coffee, etc.

In preparing the service, they need to be aware of the theme of the service and the suggested readings, discussing the make-up of the service with the speaker and contacting the music co-ordinator to discuss the theme and nature of the service and agree who is choosing music. It is sensible to produce a service plan that enables everyone involved to know what is required of them and when it will be in the service (including the music co-ordinator, OHP operator and preacher).

During the service itself, the leader has the task of holding the different elements together and this involves careful concentration! Often, there will be elements which are forced into the service which do not appear to fit – it is the job of the leader to try and ensure as good a 'fit' as possible with the minimal amount of force!

Some 'Do's' and 'Don'ts'
Do be lively, but **Don't** be over the top
Do try and make connections, but **Don't** be contrived
Do allow space for God to speak and people to think, but **Don't** let the pace drop
Do be prepared for the unexpected, but **Don't** make the service too slick

(ii) The music co-ordinator

The music co-ordinator in many churches will be the organist or music director and they may well be the best person to co-ordinate music at an all-age service. But it is often useful to involve others, especially in the choice of the songs. There is always a desire for quality in church music but what is perceived as 'quality' can be quite a subjective matter. The choice and balance of songs, as well as that of musicians, can be a divisive issue that is hard to resolve. It is, therefore, useful to ensure that an honest dialogue takes place between those running the service and those involved in the wider music of the church, so that opinions about musical styles can be aired before the service begins. Having been in a church where at one time a barrier the size of the Berlin Wall existed between the regular church choir and the all-age service music group, I can witness to the need for this to be discussed!

The role of the music coordinator is to agree with the service leader at the beginning of the week on the number and nature of the songs required as well as who is choosing them. It is preferably a joint decision, with input from both sides – but there is also a need to decide who checks that all the required acetates are available. In choosing songs, it is vital to be aware of the make-up of the congregation: making the songs accessible to children, with at least one song specifically 'aimed' at them is vital – as is including songs that allow the adults to worship in their style, possibly including a traditional hymn as the last song in the service.

Involving the children and young people in the music can be rewarding, although the music will inevitably be different from usual and will take preparation, such as photocopying of music and possible transposing of music for some instruments.

Communication is vital – meeting and praying with the service leader before the service, checking on last-minute thoughts and changes to the running order is as important as being aware of the way God is working in the service and being prepared for the service leader to make changes during the service.

(iii) The speaker

Again, communication is vital – if the service leader is the person who holds the various elements of the service together, with the overall point of the service firmly in their mind, then the speaker needs to be aware of the message which they are aiming to convey. This is not to say that the speaker does not have an input: discussions between the service leader and the speaker will help to shape what the overall message actually is. It is entirely possible (and hoped for!) that during his or her preparation, new facets of this message will appear in the speaker's mind, and this may continue during the talk itself. But the speaker must be aware of the constraints in which they work: the talk is often, though not always, the focal part of the service, but God can speak through every aspect of the service and the talk, whilst key, must not become the only thing that matters.

I would suggest that the talk lasts around 8 minutes and certainly no longer than 10. If we are talking about one major concept or idea that you are hoping that those present will take away, be challenged about and apply in their lives, then 8 minutes is long enough to tell a story and apply it in this way. Any longer and I guarantee that even the most gifted storyteller or children's speaker will struggle to maintain attention – particularly when there might be half-a-dozen toddlers on the rampage.

The main feature of a good all-age talk is that the strands of thought that run through the 45 minutes come together into one idea. The idea has been introduced, illustrated in the sung worship, introduced in detail through the reading and may have been illuminated further by some drama, but it is the job of the speaker to lay it on a plate. At first sight, it may look as though it is his or her job to dice the ingredients into fine parts – but it is not necessarily so.

The best meals do not leave you bloated but comfortably satisfied with the taste still lingering. Unfortunately, some all-age talks leave the listener either bloated with excessive length or by having offered a richness of information or style that leaves the listener struggling to cope. Think of the talk as a pudding (I like to!), a pudding that requires a balance of ingredients in itself and need some complementary elements. For example, in the same way that a very rich chocolate pudding requires ice cream or something similar to achieve a balance, so a talk needs light and shade, varying pace, visual and non-visual elements. It will take a considerable amount of trial and error to get all-age talks up to a good standard – the fact that there are so many TV cookery programmes suggests that the same is true for puddings. But it is great fun trying!

(iv) The person doing Intercessions

Intercessions are a key element of any all-age service but provide opportunities for several problems as they are often led by a member of the congregation and can be left a long way down the list in the preparation of the service. It is vital that the carefully selected person doing them knows that they must keep them short, simple and to the point. At their best, the intercessions can be stimulating and thought-provoking – at their worst, they can be a guaranteed cure for insomnia!

The intercessions usually happen towards the end of the service and, by their very nature, require an element of spontaneity, picking up on the themes (planned or unplanned) that have materialised already in the service. If the person doing them has been picking up on this, they may well feel 'inspired' to offer their own contributions to proceedings and an additional 10-minute sermon follows. There is a need for discipline: one or two short sentences relating to what has been said is entirely appropriate, but no more.

It is not unreasonable to suggest that the total length of the intercessions should be no more than 3 or 4 minutes, concluding with the Lord's Prayer (a prayer which sums up all the themes of intercession). There is a variety of ways that intercessions can be structured:

- a set of three or four prayers, focusing from world issues, through national issues to the needs of the parish
- a responsive litany, covering the same areas, but with the children actively encouraged to be involved with the responses (using language that is accessible to them)
- a family saying the prayers between them, using contributions from all the ages, representing the needs each perceives in the world and the church
- a short time of open prayer, guided by the leader. This can be highly effective if the leader sets the agenda sensitively and encourages the participants to make their contributions no more than one sentence!

The intercessions require a sense of peace and so a candle could be lit as an encouragement – this is what many schools do as part of their collective worship, so the children may well be used to the idea. Equally, the service leader may need to encourage the children to sit with their parents or be quiet where they are.

Intercessions are often overlooked as to what they can offer to a service or what they need to make them effective. Some constructive yet simple changes can make an incredible difference.

How you can begin

Resources

Unless you have some quite remarkable and gifted people in your congregation, changing or launching an all-age service is often the most difficult aspect of the job. Quite apart from identifying and preparing people to take different parts of the service, trying to find the resources to put on the service can be a hard task. Fortunately, there is an increasing volume of resource material from publishers such as Kevin Mayhew, CPAS, Scripture Union and many more. An excellent book to help you identify what is right for you and your congregation is *Seen and Heard* by Jackie Cray (Monarch Publications) which takes a much broader look at the subjects I have covered in this short introduction. Many Church of England Dioceses have resource centres and run training days for this type of worship (as do organisations like CPAS and SU).

Having the resources does not, however, take away the need to use your imagination. God gave this to each of us in order that we might be able to explore the awesome nature of his personality and love for us: our rational, finite minds are unable to comprehend the infinite God we worship and our imagination is a vital tool in trying to expand our understanding. All-age worship enables us to convey the hardest of concepts in a dynamic and wonderful way, but it requires us to use our imagination. For many adults, the imagination that made the *Famous Five* real and living in a street near us has been replaced by the cold reality of newspapers and the Internet – but our imagination is unlikely to have been lost for ever: if we can take the resources available to us and play with them to find what resonates with us and (as important) those in our congregation, we have the chance to engage in some quite dynamic worship!

And finally . . . just do it

I am hopeless at reading instruction manuals – in my opinion they are for wimps! If I get a new toy, I want to get the box open and play with it and only refer to the manual if it goes wrong. 'Learning the hard way' has its benefits, as does being sensible and reading the books first – but the best way is to do both. The service resources here are aimed at providing the basis for you to produce *your* all-age service for *your* congregation. No one knows them better than you and no one can tell you how to do it. Go out, and in the words of a well-known advert 'Just Do It!'

By doing it, you will find out what has gone wrong and learn from your mistakes. The chances are that a simple 'lifting' of other people's resources will result in something good but is less than 100 per cent relevant to your congregation. So be creative, be adventurous, be dynamic, don't be fearful . . . Just Do It!

The Services and how to use them...

The following 12 services have been designed to offer as much flexibility as possible and will enable people to fit things into the way their services already run – or to build complete services around them using the 'Service of the Word' already mentioned. This is loosely based around Year B of the Common Worship Lectionary but may also be applied to readings from other years. In some cases, the tradition of the church means that it will involve a Holy Communion service and this will not be a problem as the elements contained in the service work as well in a Eucharistic setting as in a non-Eucharistic setting. It should, however, be noted that the Eucharistic elements of the service need to be sympathetic to the all-age sense of the service as a whole – Common Worship Eucharistic Prayers D, E or H have far more accessible language than, say, A or B. It should also be noted that the ideas that follow are just that – 'ideas' which can be adapted or changed to fit the setting, the congregation or the nature of the service. The songs suggested for the services may work with some churches better than others: every church has the songs which are known and loved, but it is important that new songs are learnt which apply to new generations of worshippers.

Ultimately, the services must be owned by those who lead and speak at them and that is why there is a large element of generality about some of the items. Each service is a unique act of worship that must express the emotions, the thanks and praise, the needs and hurts, and the hearts' desires of those present. Each service is an offering to the congregation and to God and therefore needs time and prayer in preparation.

Each service has a **Title** and a **Reading**. This may be helpful as a name-tag for the service and could be used on posters and publicity.

The three questions that were asked earlier then follow: with an answer based on the thinking of the person who prepared the material. If you chose to amend this service to your own plans and needs, then these questions still need to be answered – and the answers may be different!

- **What is the one thing you want them to take away?**
- **What is the one issue you want to challenge them about?**
- **What is the one thing you want them to apply in their lives?**

A short introduction follows that tries to explain the thinking behind the service and how it might fit into the church's year.

Preparing the church

As has been mentioned already, the twenty-first century is characterised by a generation that is far more visually-based in its learning than previous generations. Moving the church around or displaying pictures relating to ideas in the service to follow can, therefore, be a great help in the conveying of concepts. At the same time, there are other preparations that often need to be thought about in advance and these are also mentioned under this heading.

Beginning

All services need a beginning and this may be just one suggestion. The important thing is that the leader is himself or herself and that any welcome is not 'forced'. Equally, avoid any habitual greeting that might be amusing once or twice but can be cringingly embarrassing for those who have seen or heard it several dozen times before!

Songs

Some songs that may be suitable for the theme of the service are suggested. *The Source* and *The Source 2,* published by Kevin Mayhew, offer a vast range of songs and hymns and contain many of these suggested songs.

Short talk and Teaching

A short talk is included which can either be placed near the beginning to introduce the theme or concept of the service or become part of the main talk itself. The main talk may take several different forms and should take no more than 10 minutes as an absolute maximum – often it is hard to time them as the responsive element may either take 30 seconds or five minutes, but the teaching element will usually take no more than five minutes.

Prayer of Repentance and Statement of what we believe

Suggestions as to which are used (both from *Common Worship*) follow, possibly with some idea of how they might be explained to those present.

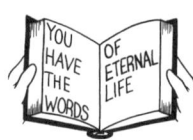

Bible reading

A Bible reading is suggested – usually a Gospel reading. The reading is one of the *Common Worship* Year B Lectionary readings and other readings may be added as necessary.

Intercessions and Lord's Prayer

Some suggestions as to how the Intercessions might be structured are also added.

Ending

As with the beginning, a good and effective ending is vital and some suggestions are made (with the assumption that some form of prayer of Blessing will also be used.)

Advent Sunday
Look out! (Luke 21:25-36)

- **What is the one thing you want them to take away?**
- ✓ That life is not supposed to be lived in fear, but with a background awareness that Jesus will return one day as he has promised to do.
- **What is the one issue you want to challenge them about?**
- ✓ Are you prepared for Jesus to return?
- **What is the one thing you want them to apply in their lives?**
- ✓ That keeping alert is part of the Christian life

The promise of Jesus that he would return one day is not an 'optional' aspect of the Christian creed but one that the church hangs on to, anticipating the event that will bring God's plan for his creation to completion. Being aware (as opposed to worrying or fearing) that the event could happen at any time is part of Christian discipleship.

Preparing the church

Put some suitable road signs around the church (available on the Internet or on many graphics programs). These should include 'warning' signs as well as a variety of types of signs.

Beginning

Welcome with a reminder that we are on a journey through life. While we are at different stages on that journey, we travel together as a church.

Songs

Songs with an expectation of Jesus' return, such as 'I cannot tell', 'Soon and very soon' or 'Great is the darkness' are appropriate but make sure you include a song that is directly relevant to the children – it doesn't have to have an Advent theme but must have a positive lyric.

Short talk

Point out the signs in church and ask what each one means. Relate it to the Christian life and point out the similarities (e.g. 'No Entry' – things we shouldn't do, 'Bend' – a change of direction in life, etc.). Produce one more sign (OHP 1), a warning sign: 'Jesus will return', and explain what it means. Say this is a sign we need to be aware of in our Christian lives and we'll talk more about it later.

Prayer of Repentance

Say that we need to acknowledge that we have been so busy living in this world that we have failed to see the signs God gives us and have not made time to think of the return of Jesus. The Confession 'Resurrection... etc.' on page 125 of *Common Worship* would be appropriate with the first Absolution on page 137.

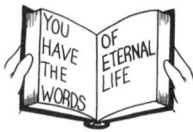

Bible reading

Read Luke 21:25-36 using a modern translation.

Teaching

The speaker should sit in the body of the Congregation (unless they are the clergy). The talk begins with the end of the reading and the leader introducing an unprepared speaker:

Leader Thanks for that reading. Time for the talk now... Speaker *(name)*... Speaker...

Speaker Is it me!

Leader Yes... you're speaking this morning. Didn't you know?

Speaker Are you sure?

Leader It was on the rota.

Speaker But I haven't planned anything... I'm not sure what I'm supposed to be talking about... What *am* I talking about?

Leader Being ready.

The speaker then comes forward with a briefcase containing a diary, a mobile phone, a set of keys and a wooden cross.

Explain that you'll have to come as you are because you didn't read the rota – and that all you can offer people is what you have with you in your bag:

A diary – You could tell people about all the things you have done.

A mobile phone – You could tell people about all the places you look for help and the people you know.

A set of keys – You could tell people about your car, your house and all the things you have which are yours and you have worked for.

But you wouldn't have very much that's exciting to talk about. You see, you didn't see the signs and so weren't ready when the time came for you to do something important.

The last thing that Jesus said before he went back to heaven was that one day he would return and the reading from the Bible talks about signs (some of them quite scary) that would tell people that he was going to return. Some of those signs have already happened and we believe that Jesus could come back one day soon.

The important question is, **Would you be ready to meet Jesus if he were to come back today?**

Some people will meet Jesus with a list of all the things they've done (**diary**), they will have lots of people who will tell Jesus that they were a nice person (**phone**), and they will have a list of all the things they achieved (**keys**).

But **all the things** we've done, the **people we've met** and the **things we've accumulated** don't mean very much. There's one more thing in your bag (**cross**). This is the one thing which enables you to be ready to meet Jesus – whenever he comes. All of the other things (**diary, phone and keys**) tell me what **you've done**.

The cross tells you what Jesus did. When we meet Jesus, when he comes back again, as he promised he would, we will be unprepared if we think that we can be with him for eternity because of anything we have done. It is only by hanging on (**tight**) to what he has done for you that we can be sure.

When some people go on a journey, they are scared that they will lose their ticket and so they keep checking that it is where they have put it. Even though they know it is safe, they keep checking and don't enjoy the journey because of it.

God doesn't want us to live each day, worrying that we won't be ready. He wants us to live knowing that because of what Jesus did (**cross**) our ticket is safe if we trust in him.

He showed how much God loved us and how much God wanted us to be ready, freed from all the wrong things we do, so that we can be with him for ever.

You hope we're all ready.

Statement of what we believe

Explain that the return of Jesus is not something we have added to what we believe but is an important part of what Christians believe. Remind everyone that Jesus went back to be with God his Father after the resurrection and is reigning there with him, waiting for the day when he comes back to earth. The Affirmation of Faith number 4 on page 147 of *Common Worship* is ideal.

Intercessions and Lord's Prayer

Include prayers that look at the world, national and local situations and ask God to help people involved to improve them. Recognise Jesus' promise to return and ask him to help everyone in church be ready for it.

Ending

If you plan to finish with a traditional hymn, 'Hark the glad sound' or 'O come, O come, Emmanuel' might be appropriate. Explain that the words encourage us to look forward to Jesus' return – Jesus has assured us that if we trust in him, we need not worry about these things. Conclude with a prayer to ask God to give us that confidence.

OHP 1

Christmas Day

Unwrapping Christmas (Luke 2:1-14)

- **What is the one thing you want them to take away?**
✓ That Christmas is part of the Easter story.

- **What is the one issue you want to challenge them about?**
✓ That the true meaning of Christmas needs to be found under lots of wrapping.

- **What is the one thing you want them to apply in their lives?**
✓ To remember the meaning of Christmas Day amid everything else.

By the time people get to Christmas morning, they have probably heard the story retold several times. The need to give the story an 'angle' must also consider the need for it to be heard in a simple and straightforward way as those who attend will be expecting it to be so. There are also likely to be visitors needing to be considered so this service tries to maintain a balance between the fun and joy of Christmas and the wonder at its part in the overall story of Salvation. The talk contains a reference to Holy Communion, in that many churches have a Communion service on Christmas morning – this, however, can be removed for the talk without changing the sense of the talk.

Preparing the church

An OHP with the words 'Welcome to Christmas!' will help to set the tone of the service. The main feature of the service is the 'pass the parcel' in the talk. This needs careful preparation in that each layer needs to be covered with fairly strong paper and contain the 'surprise' or 'expected' statement and, if thought appropriate, a sweet of some kind. Ensure your organist or music group can play something suitably Christmassy (and child-friendly) during the 'pass the parcel' or use a Christmas CD. The prize at the centre should be a box of miniature Easter eggs which are now available all year round(!). Make sure you have more than enough to go round and it may be better to line the box (such as a Chinese takeaway container) with tissue paper to stop the eggs rattling.

Beginning

A simple welcome to the service is all that is required as those who have come have an idea of what to expect!

Songs

Even though they have been sung several times in the run-up to Christmas Day, the traditional carols such as 'Hark, the herald-angels' and 'O little town of Bethlehem' are still very popular. It is a good idea to include one for the youngest present, such as 'Away in a manger' and invite them to sing the first verse on their own (maybe with your help if necessary). 'Silent night' and 'Come and join the celebration' are other good choices as is 'O come, all ye faithful' to finish the service – especially as it is often the only chance people get to sing the last verse!

Short talk

Use the traditional Christmas morning questions...
Who has opened a present already today? Who hasn't?
Who was awake earliest? Who woke up their parents?
Get the children (and the adults) to show the presents they have brought to church. Ask whether anyone has not had an opportunity to open a present yet. Ask whether they have any idea what presents they might get. Say that we'll come back to think more about presents later in the service.

Prayer of Repentance

The Christmas Confession on page 123 of *Common Worship* is suitable, as is the first or second Absolution on page 135.

Bible reading

Read Luke 2:1-14 using a modern translation – it is a reading that will have been read at several carol services and so using a paraphrase such as *The Message* or *The New Living Bible* may give it a different feel.

Teaching

Referring to someone (possibly an adult) who has told you of an opened present in the earlier talk, ask:
When you opened your present, did you know what was inside?
Did you have an idea of what to expect?
Anyone had a surprise present?

The thing about the meaning of Christmas is that *we* know what to expect from it, because we've heard it all before. Mary and Joseph knew they were going to have a baby and they knew he was going to be called Jesus but there were going to be plenty of surprises.

We're going to play 'pass the parcel' with a difference – it's called 'Expected or Surprise'. We're going to pass the parcel, gradually unwrapping the layers until we get to the big prize in the middle. In the same way that we tear the wrapping off Christmas presents to find out what's inside, we need to take the wrapping off Christmas to find out what is really inside at the heart of Christmas.

A practical note – ensure the parcel gets passed around as much of the church as possible and stops with people of all ages. This may be easier said than done in some churches!

Each layer of the parcel has something to do with Christmas – the question is: 'Is this thing expected or a surprise?'

- Mary was going to have a baby **(Expected)**
- The baby was going to be born in Bethlehem **(Expected)**
- Shepherds and wise men turned up to see the baby **(Surprise)**
- When they took Jesus to the Temple, an old lady called Anna and an old man called Simeon said amazing things about the baby **(Surprise)**
- The baby would grow up to perform miracles and teach people about God **(Surprise and Expected)**
- One day, the baby would die and rise again **(Surprise)**
- With prize: The baby was a gift to be shared with the whole world! **(Surprise)**

Ask the 'winner' to answer the question before opening the prize and then to guess what they think the prize might be.

The biggest surprise is that Easter is at the heart of Christmas. Some people wonder why we have Communion on Christmas Day. It is a good question: the answer is that Christmas is not an event all on its own. Christmas is part of the Easter story and Easter is part of the Christmas story.

When we unwrap Christmas, we find the best present of all: a baby who would grow up to die for the sin of the whole world and rise from the dead to give the whole world a chance of life – now *that* is a present!

Statement of what we believe

Explain that working out how Christmas came to be part of the whole story of God's love for us was something people in the early church struggled with. Use the Affirmation of Faith number 4 on page 147 of *Common Worship*, saying that this was a way they explained it soon after Jesus rose from the dead.

Intercessions and Lord's Prayer

Give thanks to God for the surprises of Christmas and include prayers for those who will have no surprises or presents as well as those who will have a surprise because others have given up Christmas to work in a soup kitchen or Christmas shelter. It would be possible to base the prayers round the themes in the confession already used in the service.

Ending

As people go from the service, invite them to thank God for the best present of all when they sit down to lunch – and if they have presents still to unwrap, to do so, remembering God's gift to the world.

New Year

God is in charge (Psalm 148)

- **What is the one thing you want them to take away?**
✓ That God has plans for the year ahead.

- **What is the one issue you want to challenge them about?**
✓ What do you want to do with the coming year?

- **What is the one thing you want them to apply in their lives?**
✓ To make the most of the new start a new year offers.

The reading is for the First Sunday of Christmas – traditionally a Sunday when many people are away or on holiday and as a result, churches do not run separate children's activities, giving an opportunity to put on a simple and readily accessible service for all ages. This service relies upon minimal preparation (an advantage given the busyness of the previous weeks) whilst offering an opportunity to pause at the turn of the year. Certain references to New Year's resolutions may be in advance or in retrospect, depending on the relative position of the service to New Year's day. The basic idea is that the congregation has an opportunity to privately express their regrets for the year just ended and (if required) publicly express their desires for the year to come. It is something which is truly 'all age' as it is aimed at the whole congregation rather than simply the children, but the children may require adult help to think about the ideas.

Preparing the church

The key elements of preparation are two different-coloured pads of sticky memo notes. Ensure there are enough for one of each colour for everyone in the congregation (as well as something to write with). A large clip frame, A4 or A3 size, depending on the size of the congregation, would be useful to display one set of memo notes – perhaps displayed in a hallway or to be placed somewhere a faculty is not required! A flip chart is also useful, or an OHP equipped with an acetate that can be written on. For the start of the service, if an OHP is available, turn it on but without an acetate on it (i.e. so that just the light shows).

Beginning

Welcome the congregation, hoping that they have recovered from the Christmas celebrations and are ready for a new year. See if anyone notices that the OHP does not have anything on it and say that you start the service in the same way that you will start the new year – with a blank piece of paper and that you want God to fill it. So the question for today is, 'What do you want to do with the coming year?' (OHP 1)

31

Songs

Songs which reflect the glories of Psalm 148 include 'Let everything that has breath', 'Great in power', 'My Jesus, my Saviour', 'Who paints the skies?', and the quieter 'Faithful One'. 'This is the day' could be used, too, with the words 'This is the year' inserted. The hymn 'Lord for the years' is very suitable to finish with, especially as it is long enough to allow everyone to bring forward their sticky memos!

Short talk

Has anyone made a New Year's resolution? Anyone prepared to admit to it? Can anyone remember the resolution they made last year? Did anyone keep it all year? How long was the longest resolution kept? The great thing about a new year is that it gives a chance to start afresh and try again to do things which we didn't do last year.

We don't need to wait for a new year to go back to God and start again – we can do that at any time because of what Jesus did for us on the cross. However, a new year gives us an opportunity to think about what we did wrong during the past year and to ask God to help us change things in our lives in the coming year.

Say that before you come to the confession, you're going to have a small time of quiet during which people can think of anything in their lives which they would like to change in the year to come. Ask the music group to play quietly (or play a quiet tape or CD) for about a minute and then invite people (if they wish) to write something of what they have been thinking on the memo they have been given and to take it home and stick it in their Bible as a reminder. Now you come to a . . .

Prayer of Repentance

Suggest that as people pray the Confession they also ask God to help them with the thing written on their memo. Use the Confession for Resurrection on page 125 and the fourth Absolution on page 135 of *Common Worship*.

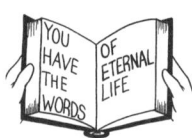
Bible reading

Read Psalm 148 using a modern translation. This could be read by one person (preferably in an enthusiastic manner!) or could be read by two (or more) people spread around the church.

Teaching

Have you ever had a moment when you looked at the world and thought 'Wow!!' Maybe you were standing on a mountain top, or lying on your back in a field looking up at the night sky or maybe simply walking along the road. Psalm 148 tells of someone doing just that – and realising that when we look around us we can see that God has given us a world to live in which is amazing. Wherever this person looked, they saw things which said 'God is amazing' – (OHP 2).

But these things also said that because God had made the world and everything and everyone in it, then he is also in charge and in control of it. So we don't have to worry about the year about to start because God knows what is going to happen.

Back to the big question (OHP 1) – we've already said the things which we want God to change in our lives. The next question is to ask what God wants to happen in our church in the coming year. There are lots of things and people to pray for – but what would you like to pray for? What are the things that you would like to see happen in your church which would be good for everyone? *Prepare in advance a checklist (for your own reference) of the sort of areas or people in church life who need prayer and reflect the agenda of the leadership – be prepared that some other agendas may be offered, but may be worded in ways that make them less controversial!*

Ask for some ideas and write them on the flip chart or OHP. Say that this is not the only set of ideas but a chance to share them. Once you have sufficient ideas, invite people to write their own brief prayer of just a few words on the second sticky memo they have been given. It may be something on the list or something completely different – but it must be *their* prayer. Ask the musicians to play for a minute or so while people write their prayers. Once everyone has finished, suggest that they hold onto their memo or stick it on the chair in front as you'll be using it in the service later.

Statement of what we believe

The Affirmation of Faith number 7 on page 148 of *Common Worship* is appropriate.

Intercessions and Lord's Prayer

Invite people to speak out aloud the things that they have written on their memo stickers during the second talk. During the last song/hymn, invite them to come forward and place their sticky memos onto a large piece of paper (randomly).

Ending

Thank people for their contributions and tell them that they will be placed in a clip frame with the words 'The Prayers of . . . for the year . . .' in the centre of the frame. Invite people to look at the frame during the year, and next New Year you will be able to look at the prayers again and say thank you to God for the answers you have received.

OHP 1

The BIG Question...

What do you want to do with the coming year?

OHP 2

Sun Trees Nations

Heavens People Moon

Weather

Birds Mountains

GOD IS AMAZING!

Stars Angels

Wildlife

Children Rulers

Sea Creatures Small Animals

Epiphany

The Light shines in the darkness (Matthew 2:1-12)

- **What is the one thing you want them to take away?**
✓ That this world can be a dark place and needs the Light of the World.
- **What is the one issue you want to challenge them about?**
✓ Are you making the most of the Light?
- **What is the one thing you want them to apply in their lives?**
✓ That the light shines in *every* place.

The arrival of the wise men to see the infant Jesus was a sign that the Saviour was for the whole world – that the light would shine across every continent and nation. Epiphany coincides with the traditional end of the Christmas celebration – and is often lost in thoughts about a new year. Some churches use Epiphany as an opportunity to put on a Christingle Service and some of the ideas in this service could easily be adapted to work in such a service.

Preparing the church

The key aim of the service is to contrast light and darkness. Various ideas involving images of light can be used as people come into church. If a data projector is available, then pictures of light (e.g. candles, the sun, coloured lights, etc.) could be used. If a television is available, a video of a candle in a dark room could be very effective – as would a simple acetate or picture of a candle. Quiet background music is an effective way of adding to the atmosphere. The use of candles in the service may be unusual for some, but can be a great visual aid – especially if none are lit at the start of the service. The speaker will need to have a powerful torch and a mirror.

Beginning

Once everyone is in church, turn off all the lights (the darker you can get the church, the better!) and, ensuring the speaking voice is as prominent as possible, read Genesis 1:1-3, before a candle (the bigger, the better) is lit in the centre of the church. Once it is lit, John 1:9 is read, and (if possible) go straight into the first song, during which further candles can be lit and the church lights gradually switched on (a good idea, especially if the congregation are using hymn books!).

Songs

'As with gladness, men of old' is a traditional hymn that fits with the theme and reading, but more modern songs which mention Jesus as the Light of the World are useful as are songs such as 'Be still, for the presence of the Lord', 'Darkness, like a shroud', 'Like a candle flame', 'O Jesus, Son of God' and the traditional 'Angel voices ever singing'. 'Shine, Jesus, shine' may be appropriate as a song with which to finish the service.

Short talk

Talk about the fact that in Britain we very rarely experience true darkness because of the amount of street lighting available to us. If there is someone in the congregation who has worked in places where this is not the case, ask them about it, or ask someone who remembers the 'winter of unrest' and the power workers' strikes of the early '70s! Ask the children about our need for light – however dim – and what happens if we don't have it.

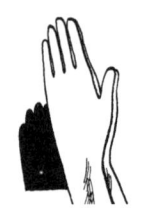

Prayer of Repentance

The *Common Worship* Confession for Resurrection, etc. on page 125 is appropriate, along with the last Absolution on page 136.

Bible reading

Using a modern translation, read Matthew 2:1-12. One way of making this more visual would be to place readers around the church and have three wise men move around the church. They process up an aisle towards Jerusalem and are met by Herod, before moving on to Mary and Joseph (by the crib, if conveniently placed) and then returning down the aisle, avoiding meeting Herod on the way. Most of the costumes will have been used at a recent nativity play and this can be a help in the children's understanding of the story.

Teaching

Begin by asking some questions about the story:

- How did the wise men know that a baby had been born? (A star.)
- How did the chief priests and teachers know where Jesus would be born? (From their Bible, the Old Testament.)
- How did the Wise Men know they had arrived? (Because the star stopped over the stable.)

Put up OHP 1 with the words 'They found their way using the light of the star'. Ask if anyone had a torch for Christmas and if they have used it. Ask for the lights to be switched off and ask how easy it is to see your way around the church (answers will vary from church to church – if need be, ask how easy it would be to find your way around the church at night!) Produce a torch (the more powerful the better) and ask what difference this makes. Then ask what else can you do with the torch, aiming for answers such as:

- See obstructions that might cause you to trip up.
- See people's faces rather than just hearing their voices.
- Send signals in Morse Code.

- Look ahead of you to see what is in the distance, not just nearby.
- See dirt and cobwebs in the roof of the church (but be sensitive to any cleaners present!).

Ask for the lights to be put back on again and say that today is Epiphany (or mention which day it was/will be) and that the word comes from a Greek word *epiphaneia* which means 'to show forth'. Epiphany is a time when we remember how the wise men came from afar to see Jesus and that it showed that Jesus didn't come just for the people of Israel but for the whole world.

Jesus said in John 8:12 'I am the light of the world. Whoever follows me will never walk in darkness, but will have the light of life.' (OHP 2) Remind people that if Jesus is the Light of the World, then it means he will be there to do the same things in our lives as our torch:

- See obstructions – to help us see things in life which are not good for us.
- See people's faces – to help us see people as he sees them.
- Send signals – to understand what God wants for us.
- Look ahead of you – to know that he has a plan for our lives.
- See dirt and cobwebs – to help us see the things in our lives that need changing.

It may be good to mention Psalm 119:105 'Your word is a lamp to my feet and a light for my path.'

Finally, remind people that you began your service with the words: 'The true light that gives light to every man was coming into the world' and that we light candles in church to remind ourselves that the Light of the World has come into the world – and is still with us by the presence of the Holy Spirit. The wise men found their way to Jesus by the light of the star but we are told went home rejoicing and praising God – not because of the light of the star but (OHP 3) because 'They found their way using the star of the Light'.

Spend a few moments in quiet and encourage everyone (whatever age) to concentrate on the big candle at the front of church, asking God for Jesus' light to shine in our hearts – then pray a short prayer asking God to do that.

Statement of what we believe

The Affirmation of Faith 7 on page 148 of *Common Worship* is appropriate.

Intercessions and Lord's Prayer

Taking recent news items from across the world, in the nation and from your own community, ask that the light of Jesus will shine into each of those situations.

A final thought

Before you sing the final song ('Shine, Jesus, shine' is the suggested song), ask one simple question – how can the light of Jesus shine in your life? Take the mirror (about A4 size would be preferable) and give it to someone in the congregation – and shine your torch at it. Offer the thought that if we let Jesus into our lives then his love will shine out through everything we say or do – his love will reflect in us.

Ending

Paul encouraged the Philippians to 'Shine like stars' – pray that the light of Jesus will shine out in each person's life like a star in the coming week.

They found their way using the light of the star

*I am the light of the world.
Whoever follows me
will never walk in darkness,
but will have the light of life.*
John 8:12

Light helps us to . . .
- See obstructions
- See people's faces
- Send signals
- Look ahead
- See the dirt!

*Your word is a lamp to my feet
and a light for my path.*
Psalm 119:105

OHP 3

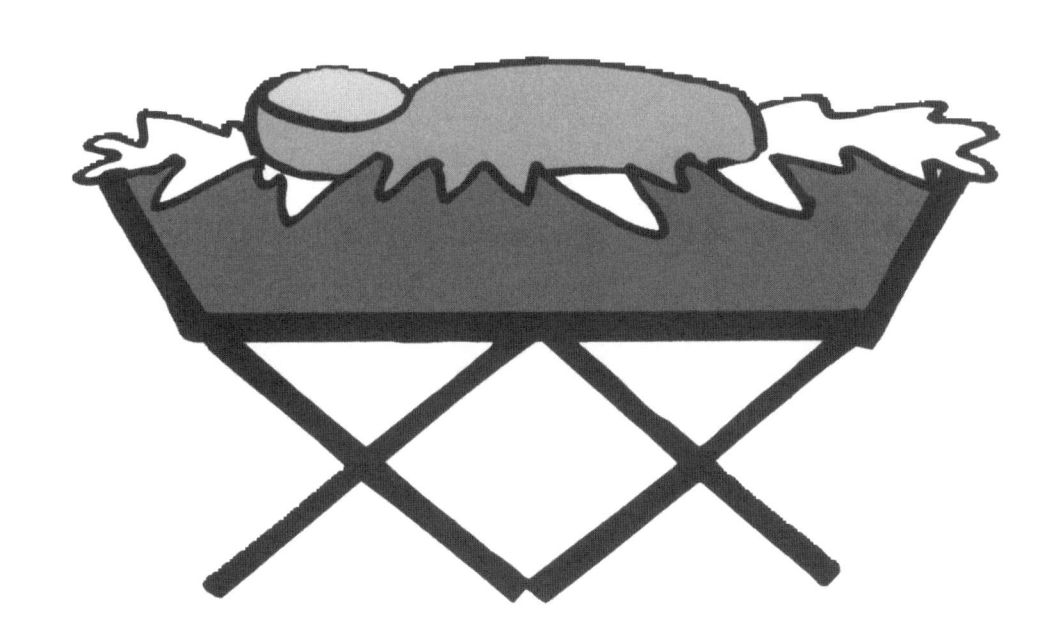

They found their way using the star of the Light

Ash Wednesday / First Sunday in Lent

Oops – I did it again (Matthew 4:1-11)

- **What is the one thing you want them to take away?**
✓ We are all tempted – but being tempted is not the same as sinning.

- **What is the one issue you want to challenge them about?**
✓ Could we resist temptation more often than we do?

- **What is the one thing you want them to apply in their lives?**
✓ We can stand up to temptation – because Jesus did.

Temptation is something every single person faces every single day of their life. When we read of Jesus being tempted, we may think that it was the only time it happened and that he simply shrugged it off ('Well, he was God, wasn't he?'). We forget that in Gethsemane, the temptation to walk away and live a normal life was so great that his sweat was like blood. The most helpful thing for anyone involved in this service to do is to stop and acknowledge to God (if not to each other) that all of us are tempted – and all too often we give in. An aspect of Lent that many struggle with is the idea of giving something up: this service tries to approach Lent with the idea of doing something positive as well – such as a daily prayer time or joining a house group.

Preparing the church

If you have a Lord's Table that is visible from the whole church, place on it lots of things in daily life and the sort of things which people may give up for Lent: a newspaper, a book, bottle of wine, a jar of coffee, a bar of chocolate, a video or DVD, etc. Also put onto it a Bible and a Prayer Book. If the Lord's Table is not visible from everywhere, then try and create a 'temporary' Lord's Table by covering a table at the front of the church with a cloth and place a cross (and candles if appropriate) as well as the items mentioned above.

Beginning

Welcome people and remind them that we are in Lent. The word 'Lent' comes from a German word '*lenz*', which means 'Spring' and we traditionally associate spring with new life and good things. It is strange, therefore, that when we think of Lent, we associate it with having to give things up!

Songs

'What a friend we have in Jesus' is a hymn accessible to children and could be used. Lent is not a time we would normally associate with joyful songs, but 'We want to see Jesus lifted high', 'Who paints the skies?' or 'I once was frightened of spiders' provide opportunities to remind us that we needn't be afraid or worry about these things because God is with us. 'Soften my heart', 'Purify my heart' or 'Faithful One' may be used prior to the intercessions as requests or reminders of God's faithfulness to us. The new version of 'The Lord's my shepherd' is also accessible to all ages.

Short talk

Refer to the table with all the things in life and ask whether anyone has given anything up for Lent. Ask why we give things up and mention the idea of 'discipline', and that Jesus' disciples had to give some things up when they followed him. Comment that it is sometimes good to give things up for Lent as we can appreciate them more afterwards – but we don't *have* to give things up for Lent.

Prayer of Repentance

As an introduction, mention that the one thing God wants us to give up, not just for Lent but for ever, is sin. That is why we have to come back and say 'sorry' time and time again. The Confession for Lent on page 124 of *Common Worship* is appropriate.

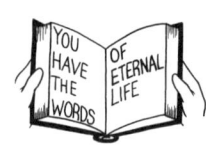

Bible reading

Read Matthew 4:1-11 from a modern translation. It could be helpful to use some pictures to illustrate the reading (e.g. some stones and loaves of bread, a picture of a cathedral and a crown).

Teaching

If you can tell a story in a humorous way, introduce the idea of temptation by telling a story, e.g. how you were trying to lose weight and when you went into a shop, all the bars of chocolate seemed to cry at you, 'Eat me!' Note that all of us are tempted every single day and we must never forget three things about temptation (OHP 1).

- Being tempted is not the same as sinning.
- Jesus was tempted like us, not just in the desert but all through his life.
- No temptation is too difficult. The Bible tells us: *God is faithful; he will not let you be tempted beyond what you can bear. But when you are tempted, he will also provide a way out so that you can stand up under it* (1 Corinthians 10:13).

So what were the temptations that Jesus faced? (OHP 2).

- Jesus was hungry, so the devil suggested he turn a stone into bread.
- Jesus had a difficult job to do, so the devil suggested he make it easy by doing something spectacular that would make everyone know, rather than just believe, that he was the Son of God.
- Jesus had given up his life of glory in heaven to come to earth, so the devil offered Jesus the chance to have everything this world could offer in return for bowing down to the devil.

How did Jesus withstand the temptation? (OHP 3).

- **Jesus knew his Bible.** The devil knew the Bible, too, and quoted bits of it at Jesus as he tempted him – but Jesus knew not just the words of the Bible but what they meant so he was able to resist. We get tempted to make up our own version of what the Bible means – e.g. 'Do not steal' does not mean 'Finders keepers'!
- **Jesus put God first.** We get tempted to think that we can 'get around' to God – that we can do other things first and we will get to God sooner or later. God wants us to think about him first – before ourselves. That way, we will not give in to the temptation.
- **Jesus actually did what God wanted.** Sometimes we get tempted to do things when we know that no one will find out – God still wants us to *do* the right thing rather than simply *think* the right thing!

During Lent, many people give things up – but often they fail to keep going. It is so easy to sneak a quick chocolate bar when you are out – after all, no one will see! One idea for Lent is that we take something up as well as give something up. For example, we might give up chocolate, but decide that we will make sure we read our Bible every single day in Lent. That way, we will be better equipped when we are tempted to eat some chocolate! Sum up the talk, using the three OHPs.

Statement of what we believe

The Creed on page 144 of *Common Worship* is appropriate for Lent.

Intercessions and Lord's Prayer

Include prayers that ask God to help us when we are tempted to remember what we have learnt in the Bible, to put God first and *always* do what he wants us to do. Pray for those who find this difficult (e.g. people in the news who have been tempted to do wrong things and have done them) and thank God for his forgiveness when we say 'sorry' to him.

Ending

Invite people to remember anything they may have decided to do during the service (e.g. take something up for Lent) and remind them it is never too late to start and they don't have to stop at Easter!

Three things about Temptation

1
Being tempted is not the same as sinning

2
Jesus was tempted like us, not just in the desert but all through his life

3
No temptation is too difficult

The Bible tells us:

And God is faithful; he will not let you be tempted beyond what you can bear. But when you are tempted, he will also provide a way out so that you can stand up under it.
1 Corinthians 10:13

OHP 2

Three things Jesus was tempted with

1
Food

2
Laziness

3
Everything in the world

How Jesus beat Temptation

1
Jesus knew his Bible

2
Jesus put God first

3
Jesus actually did what God wanted

Mother's Day
Mary – a VSM (Very Special Mum)!
(Luke 2:33-35)

- **What is the one thing you want them to take away?**
✓ That Mary was an ordinary mother given an extraordinary task.

- **What is the one issue you want to challenge them about?**
✓ Not taking motherhood for granted (as a mother or a child)

- **What is the one thing you want them to apply in their lives?**
✓ That God loves us with the tender love of a Mother.

Mother's Day has become a highly commercial day which, like Christmas, often needs unpacking in order to find its true meaning. If God is infinite, then his personality is infinite and although the Bible gives him male characteristics, everything that we know as feminine and motherly is also contained within his character. Hence the motherly desire of God to protect people, described by Jesus in Matthew 23:37. Mother's Day can be a very hard one for single people or those who have no children of their own and it is vital that the service acknowledges their role as spiritual 'Aunts' and 'Grandparents' in the family of God, without taking away from the special role that mothers play in our lives.

Preparing the church

Find pictures of as many well-known mothers as possible, e.g. the Queen, pop stars, actresses. They do not need to be known for their parenting skills, only that they are mothers. A PowerPoint presentation using a projector can be very effective, using pictures readily available on the Internet – but pasted pictures from newspapers or magazines placed around the church can be equally effective.

Beginning

As the service begins, invite everyone who has their mother with them to turn to them and say, 'Hello – and thank you for being my mum!' Then invite everyone to turn to someone female near them and say 'Hello – and thank you for being a sister/aunt/grandmother to me!'

Songs

The songs for Mother's Day revolve around God's love. A traditional hymn such as 'Love divine' will be a popular hymn with which to close the service as it is used at many weddings. Other songs that might be used include 'Men of faith (Shout to the north)', 'My Jesus, my Saviour', 'A new commandment', or 'Overwhelmed by love'. If you use 'God is good to me' as a children's song, you could add the verse 'He gave me Mum to be my chum, God is good to me!', holding hands out and then clasping them to your heart as the actions.

Short talk

Look at the pictures around the church (or the PowerPoint presentation) and ask 'What makes these mothers "good" mothers?' Be as positive as possible – even the ones who may be perceived as not being as 'good' as we think they ought to be still love their children. Note that for some it is difficult to talk about their mum as they either never knew them or lost them at some point in their lives – but ask the question 'What was the best thing about your mother or the most special person who brought you up?' Then ask, 'What sort of a child are you or were you?' and use this as a lead in to the Confession.

Prayer of Repentance

Explain that although the Bible talks about God as being our Father and that Jesus called God 'Father', there are things in the Bible that also tell us that God loves us like a mother loves her children, too. The Confession for Reconciliation on page 127 of *Common Worship* may be appropriate, although some may prefer the first Confession on page 129.

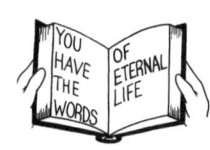

Bible reading

Read Luke 2:33-35 using a modern translation.

Teaching

If people have a Bible to hand, ask them to turn to Luke chapter 1 and then list together the stories that are in chapters 1 and 2 of the Gospel (OHP 1). Ask who is the one person who is connected to all of them. (No, it's NOT Jesus!) It is Mary.

There is a legend that while he was travelling with Paul, Luke went to Ephesus and there he met Mary, who was by this time a very old lady. Luke was writing the story of Jesus and the first two chapters of Luke's gospel are what Mary told Luke – how else could we know that Mary 'treasured all these things in her heart' (Luke 2:19, 51) unless she herself had told the person writing?

Mary was a VSM – a very special mum – because she had an important job to do. Is there anyone present who is about 30 years old? Say that you feel sure that we could sit all day listening to the story of his/her life and yet we only know one story about Jesus from the time when he was a baby until he was 30 – the story of him in the Temple aged 12. The rest of the time he grew up as a son to Mary and to Joseph and learnt to be a carpenter in the family shop.

List some of the other stories we know about Mary (OHP 2). Remind people that Mary was a mum just like every other mum – she made mistakes and learnt from Jesus just as he learnt from her. But she had a special job – to bring Jesus up and she never stopped loving him even when he said that his job was more important than being with her (Luke 8). Remind people that she saw the job through to the end and was able to rejoice with the other friends of Jesus when he rose from the dead.

Remind people again that God loves us both as our heavenly Father and also just like a mother loves her children. Mary did a wonderful job and reminds us how special the job of being a mum is and how we should always thank God for our mothers.

Statement of what we believe

The responsive form of the Apostles Creed on page 143 of *Common Worship* may be appropriate, although the Affirmation on page 144 may equally be appropriate.

Intercessions and Lord's Prayer

Include prayers for the mothers who are present as well as those not able to be present. Pray for those who never knew their mothers as well as women who have never known the joys and privileges of being a mother. You may like to include prayers for some of the mothers in the pictures at the start of the service.

Ending

Most churches make up posies of flowers to give to all the ladies of the church on Mother's Day and it is best to hand these out during the last song or hymn. Ensure that everyone gets one (including those not well enough to be there) and invite children to take them to elderly neighbours (if flower numbers permit). A small card to give out with the flowers with the words 'Thank You for being YOU!' can emphasise the message of love.

The Stories of Luke 1 and 2

An angel visits Zechariah
Gabriel visits Mary
Mary visits Elizabeth
Mary's song
John the Baptist's birth
Zechariah's song

Jesus' birth
Visit of the shepherds
Jesus is presented in the Temple
Simeon and Anna meet Jesus
The boy Jesus goes to the Temple

His mother treasured all these things in her heart.
Luke 2:19, 51

Other Stories about Mary

She went to a wedding with Jesus
(John 2)

She went to see Jesus
(Luke 8)

She was there at the cross
(John 19)

She was there after Jesus ascended
(Acts 1)

Good Friday
Making the cut (John 19:1-27)

- What is the one thing you want them to take away?
✓ That none of us are good enough to be in God's presence – but thanks to Jesus, we can be.

- What is the one issue you want to challenge them about?
✓ The complacency we often have about our sin.

- What is the one thing you want them to apply in their lives?
✓ That the forgiveness of Good Friday relies on understanding their need for that forgiveness.

The service on Good Friday is one that has suffered as the secularisation of the day has grown. It is not an easy all-age service to provide due to the perceived difficulty of communicating the suffering of the cross to children – but if they are to understand the victory of Easter, they also need to cope with the message of Good Friday.

Preparing the church

Having a large wooden cross around on Good Friday is always helpful (there may be one available for use on a walk of witness which may follow the service). For this service, you will need an OHP and a wastepaper bin, preferably on a small table (in front of a cross, if possible). Everyone is handed a small scorecard and a pencil as they enter (Sheet 1). A set of golf clubs placed strategically at the front of church will provide a talking point before the service and help focus on the concept!

Beginning

A welcome that reminds people that this is a difficult day and a difficult story – and presents us with a question – 'Why should it be called *Good* Friday?' It is also worth mentioning that as you meet, the world will carry on outside just like any other normal day – and that was exactly how the first Good Friday happened.

Songs

Not surprisingly, there are few songs written for Good Friday that come into the 'all age' category. In addition, there are some hymns (for example, 'There is a green hill' and 'When I survey') that are only usually sung on Good Friday and they are reasonably accessible to all ages. It is best to use a traditional hymn to start and finish the service but modern songs can also be used: 'Jesus Christ, I think upon your sacrifice', 'Come and see', 'Overwhelmed by love' and 'My Lord, what love is this?'. 'Lord, I lift your name on high' could possibly be used, but the service leader would need to emphasise the aspect of the song that applies to Good Friday. Many of the songs have a credal aspect to them.

Talk 1 – The problem

Introduce the topic of golf (e.g. mention Tiger Woods or another great golfer).

Everyone present must have played crazy golf at some time – it is very simple. Each hole can theoretically be done in one shot. We're going to play a different game of Crazy Golf today.

Everyone has a scorecard – (Sheet 1)

We'll be thinking about each hole as a different challenge in life – how good are you?

How do we score? (OHP 1)
1 – Never ever done it, 2 – Done it once or twice, 3 – Do it quite often

Let's play (OHP 2).

Hole 1 – Murder

Hopefully everyone scores a '1' on this, unless...

Jesus said that if you ever felt that you wished someone were dead then it is as though you had killed them. So maybe one or two will score 2.

Hole 2 – Forgotten about God

Have you ever realised that you have been living your life without thinking about God at all? Jesus said that the greatest commandment of all was to love God with every bit if you. If there has ever been a time when you haven't done that then maybe your score is 2 or even 3.

Hole 3 – Not spent Sunday properly

It's quite hard sometimes because lots of things now happen on a Sunday which didn't used to. But there is a commandment which says that God made Sundays special. If ever you have done something on a Sunday which you knew afterwards was not really what God wanted you to then you should score a 2 or even a 3.

Hole 4 – Really, really wanted something that wasn't yours

All of us want something – a new house, a new car, a new bike, a street scooter – and it's OK to think it would be nice to have those things. But another commandment tells us that if we really, really want these things so that we can't live without them then we are not putting God first.

Hole 5 – Stealing

No one here has, as far as I am aware, been involved in a bank robbery. But, as far as God is concerned, taking anything that isn't ours is just as bad as a bank robbery: to take a book or toy that belongs to a brother or sister, to take things from work that aren't ours – stealing means taking anything that isn't ours.

Hole 6 – Fibs

I am afraid that I won't believe anyone who puts a 1 – who never, ever tells a fib. All of us do it – I do it! God tells us to tell the truth.

OK, tot up your score: Anybody get a score of 12 or less? 6? Impossible!

In real golf, you have to hand your card in at the end of the round, witnessed by someone so you can't cheat. 'The cut' is the score you need to get if you are to continue in the game.

The cut, as far as God is concerned is 6. Every time we didn't get a '1' on our scorecard we are guilty of what is called sin.

We have a problem – unless we can get a '1' in every area of our life, God says we cannot be in his presence. Because God is perfect, only perfect people can be in his presence – we have a problem!

Song

A more modern song would be appropriate at this stage.

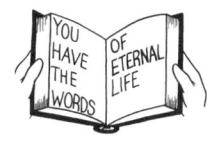

Bible reading

The lectionary reading for Good Friday is very long and it may be better to take a section (such as John 19:16b-30), using a modern translation such as *The Message*.

Talk 2 – The solution

We have a problem: our scorecards are full of 2s and 3s – we cannot make 'the cut' and we're out of the game. On your card, where it says 'Do I make the cut?' – the answer is 'no'. What do you think Jesus' scorecard looked like? The Bible tells us he never did anything wrong, so he had 1s in everything – so he *could* make the cut.

If you go to a golf course, you will find scorecards on the floor where people have given up. When Jesus said on the cross, 'It is finished', he was saying you can rip your card up and have mine, and because you have my card you can beat the cut – you can make it through to the next round (OHP 3). Read Romans 5:18.

Jesus' card is a free gift, that is why we call today 'Good' Friday. It encourages us to keep trying whilst knowing that we can come back time and time again and throw away our messed-up card and start again.

In a moment, as we sing another song bring your card up to the bin at the front: rip it up and put it in the bin, and then take one of Jesus' cards. We are saying, 'I know my performance in life will never be good enough – but thank you, Jesus, that you have given me your scorecard, and now I can be good enough to be with God.'

A quiet song

An instrumental or quiet song, performed or sung together – during which people are invited to throw their cards in the bin and take Jesus' card (Sheet 2).

Prayer of Repentance and Absolution

The responsive General Confession on page 128 of *Common Worship* and an Absolution such as the fourth one on page 136 are very appropriate.

Intercessions and Lord's Prayer

Include prayers that are aware of the sin of the whole world and thank God for the opportunity to come back and be forgiven. Include an awareness that things on a global scale, such as war and famine, are the results of selfishness and this can be true locally and individually.

Final hymn

'When I survey' is probably the best song with which to finish as it sums up the message of the service.

Ending

The service may precede a public act of witness and so it may be appropriate to have the cross (if available) lead people out of the church. There may be some for whom the discussion of sin may require further prayer. Suggest that they talk over any issues which may have been raised with the clergy or a friend.

SHEET 1

My Scorecard

Hole	Par	My Score
1	1	
2	1	
3	1	
4	1	
5	1	
6	1	
Total	6	

Do I make the cut?
Yes / No

My Scorecard

Hole	Par	My Score
1	1	
2	1	
3	1	
4	1	
5	1	
6	1	
Total	6	

Do I make the cut?
Yes / No

My Scorecard

Hole	Par	My Score
1	1	
2	1	
3	1	
4	1	
5	1	
6	1	
Total	6	

Do I make the cut?
Yes / No

My Scorecard

Hole	Par	My Score
1	1	
2	1	
3	1	
4	1	
5	1	
6	1	
Total	6	

Do I make the cut?
Yes / No

My Scorecard

Hole	Par	My Score
1	1	
2	1	
3	1	
4	1	
5	1	
6	1	
Total	6	

Do I make the cut?
Yes / No

My Scorecard

Hole	Par	My Score
1	1	
2	1	
3	1	
4	1	
5	1	
6	1	
Total	6	

Do I make the cut?
Yes / No

Jesus' Scorecard

Hole	Par	Jesus' Score
1	1	1
2	1	1
3	1	1
4	1	1
5	1	1
6	1	1
Total	6	6

Do I make the cut?   <u>Yes</u>!!!

Here it is in a nutshell: just as one person did it wrong and got us in all this trouble with sin and death, another person did it right and got us out of it. But more than just getting us out of trouble, he got us into life!

Romans 5:18 *(The Message)*

Jesus' Scorecard

Hole	Par	Jesus' Score
1	1	1
2	1	1
3	1	1
4	1	1
5	1	1
6	1	1
Total	6	6

Do I make the cut?   <u>Yes</u>!!!

Here it is in a nutshell: just as one person did it wrong and got us in all this trouble with sin and death, another person did it right and got us out of it. But more than just getting us out of trouble, he got us into life!

Romans 5:18 *(The Message)*

Jesus' Scorecard

Hole	Par	Jesus' Score
1	1	1
2	1	1
3	1	1
4	1	1
5	1	1
6	1	1
Total	6	6

Do I make the cut?   <u>Yes</u>!!!

Here it is in a nutshell: just as one person did it wrong and got us in all this trouble with sin and death, another person did it right and got us out of it. But more than just getting us out of trouble, he got us into life!

Romans 5:18 *(The Message)*

My Scorecard

Hole	Par	My Score
1	1	
2	1	
3	1	
4	1	
5	1	
6	1	
Total	6	

Do I make the cut ? Yes / No

The Scoring

1 - Never ever done it

2 - Done it once or twice

3 - Do it quite often

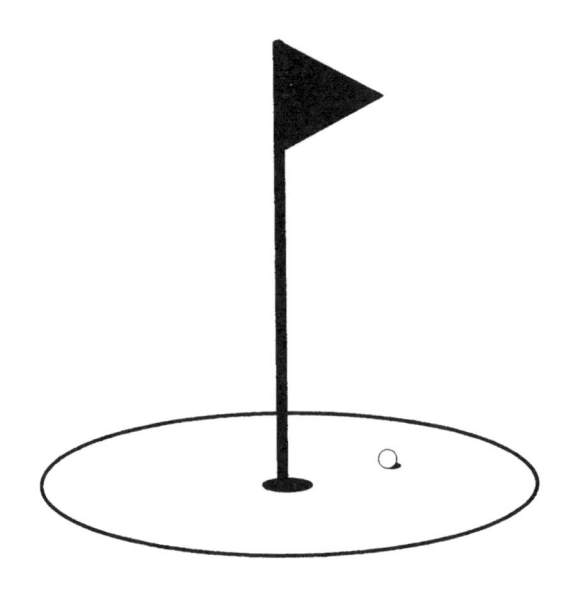

The Holes

Hole 1 - Murder

Hole 2 - Forgotten about God

Hole 3 - Not spent Sunday properly

Hole 4 - Really, really wanted something

Hole 5 - Stealing

Hole 6 - Fibs

Jesus' Scorecard

Hole	Par	Jesus' Score
1	1	1
2	1	1
3	1	1
4	1	1
5	1	1
6	1	1
Total	6	6

Do I make the cut? <u>Yes</u>!!!

Here it is in a nutshell:
just as one person did it wrong and got us in all this trouble with sin and death,
another person did it right
and got us out of it.
But more than just
getting us out of trouble,
he got us into life!

Romans 5:18 *(The Message)*

Easter Sunday

Surprise, surprise! (John 20:1-18)

- **What is the one thing you want them to take away?**
- ✓ That Easter was a surprise for everyone involved – except Jesus.
- **What is the one issue you want to challenge them about?**
- ✓ To look deeper into the Easter story.
- **What is the one thing you want them to apply in their lives?**
- ✓ To live with the excitement of Easter as a day-to-day experience.

Paul tells us in 1 Corinthians 15 that the whole Christian message stands or falls on the events of Easter Sunday. Because we know the story, we fail to realise how much of a surprise the events were – if we can be surprised, we can be excited about how important the events were.

Preparing the church

An OHP with the words 'Are you ready for a surprise?' (OHP 1) could help to set the scene as would things placed around the church that would make an amusing surprise for those attending (e.g. the vicar's most commonly used jumper hung up out of reach somewhere in the church). It would be good for the musicians to play something different as people arrive – e.g. a Christmas carol!

Beginning

The traditional Easter Greeting of 'Christ is risen!' with the response 'He is risen indeed!', said three times, with the emphasis changing each time is a great way to start the service, leading straight into the first hymn.

Songs

Traditional Easter hymns, such as 'Jesus Christ is risen today', are entirely appropriate in the all-age service, not only because they are very singable but also because there are likely to be visitors to the service who have come because it is Easter, and these are well-known hymns. More modern songs such as 'Christ is risen', 'Thank you, Jesus' are appropriate, as is the quieter 'Sing hallelujah to the Lord' which could be used as a prelude to the intercessions.

Short talk

A series of questions such as 'Who had Easter eggs – and who's eaten them already?', 'Who's eaten the most?', is interrupted by a series of surprise events: the pianist plays 'The Entertainer', a gymnast tumbles down the aisle, someone juggles, etc. When everything has quietened down – say that Easter is full of surprises and move on.

Quieter song, leading to a Prayer of Repentance

The 'Resurrection' Confession on page 125 of *Common Worship*, with the fifth Absolution on page 135 are appropriate.

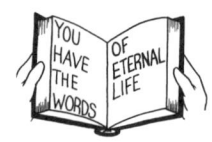

Bible reading

The reading John 20:1-18 could be taken from any modern translation and use several voices, including two narrators and voices for Jesus and Mary.

Sketch

The following sketch requires no props and no costumes – it is two ordinary people trying to explain the empty tomb. The point at which they see the risen Jesus needs careful timing and a clear understanding of the point at which they both look, and how long they look for.

The two characters wander on and look into 'something' before turning to speak.

A He's not here.

B What do you mean, he's not here?

A Like I said – he's not here.

B Well he should be.

A Well he isn't.

B All right, who's nicked him?

A Don't be daft, no one's nicked him – or didn't you see the two-ton boulder and the SAS guard out there yesterday?

B So if no one's nicked him, how did he get out?

(Pause)

A He could've pushed the stone away ... OK, silly idea.

B He could've dug a tunnel ... yep, silly.

A Well – if he didn't push it, or dig a tunnel ...

B ... and no one's nicked him.

A ... then *where is he*?

B Um ...

A So where is he?
(Pause)
They stop and both stare at the same point (person), open-mouthed.
After about five seconds, they drop to their knees.
After a further five seconds they exit (to the back) shouting 'He's alive!', 'We've seen him!', etc.

Teaching

What did you expect to see when you came to church this morning? Surprised to see different things? When Mary came to the tomb that Easter morning, what she expected to find was a dead body. The one problem she was expecting, was how to get the boulder out of the way so that she could anoint the body with the spices she and the others had brought. Mary had probably rehearsed what they were going to say to the guards to let them get on with the job. They expected to find (OHP 2):
1 – A dead body, 2 – Guards, 3 – A big stone

What did they find?
1 – No body, 2 – No soldiers, 3 – No stone in front of the tomb

They had watched Jesus die – they knew that dead people normally stay dead and weren't expecting any of this. No wonder Mary went off to find the other disciples full of confusion. It's OK for us – we know what is going to happen next in the story but Mary and the disciples didn't.

When we come to Easter – what do we expect? (OHP 3)
1 – A familiar story, 2 – Easter eggs, 3 – Daffodils, 4 – 'The Sound of Music' on TV

What can we find?
Someone who is always there – Jesus said, 'I am with you – always'.
Someone we can trust in – Jesus called Mary by name; he knows us, too.
Someone who gives life – Jesus said, 'I have come that they might have life' (John 10:10). Jesus brings hope, a future, a purpose to our lives.

Easter is full of surprises
Jesus went on surprising his friends – the disciples never knew when Jesus would appear: Emmaus/Upper Room/Lakeside. They eventually learnt that even though they couldn't see him, he was there: it is still the same for us – we may not see him, but he is here with us.

Statement of what we believe

Creed 5 on page 147 of *Common Worship* is ideal.

Intercessions and Lord's Prayer

Easter Sunday brings the hope of new life where there is despair and death: use the prayers to ask for the reality of Easter to be in these places. Ask God to help us to want and expect him to surprise us in our daily lives.

After a final hymn, an ending

After a traditional Easter Blessing, use the response:
'Go in peace to love and serve the risen Lord.'
'In the name of Christ, Amen.'

?

Are you ready for a surprise?

The women expected to find . . .

1 – A body
2 – Guards
3 – A stone

They found . . .

1 – No body
2 – No guards
3 – No stone

They were confused!

Easter: We expect to find . . .

A familiar story
Easter eggs
Daffodils
'The Sound of Music' on TV

Easter: What we can find . . .

Someone who is always there
Someone who can always be trusted
Someone who gives life

Easter . . .
. . . is full of surprises!!

Ascension

Gone but not forgotten (Acts 1:1-11)

(For Ascension Day or the Sunday after Ascension)

- **What is the one thing you want them to take away?**
✓ That Jesus *had* to go back to heaven, otherwise the Spirit could not have come.
- **What is the one issue you want to challenge them about?**
✓ Jesus' command to 'Go and make disciples' applies to us, too
- **What is the one thing you want them to apply in their lives?**
✓ Jesus promised to be with us and to send the Holy Spirit to help us in the task.

In his final teaching to the disciples recorded in John 14-17, Jesus repeatedly tries to get them to understand that his death and resurrection are part of a plan – but he goes even further and tells them that the gift of the Holy Spirit and the *real* work that God has for them to do, can only happen if Jesus went away. Nowadays, Ascension Day is one of the 'lesser' festivals in the Christian calendar but it is a vital cog in the story, one that enabled the church to actually happen.

Preparing the church

Pick an item of furniture or something in the church that is always on view and put it in the vestry or out of sight. It might be something that is obvious to you, but not so obvious to the congregation – don't make it too easy! It would be very helpful if there are Bibles to hand for the talk – most churches have pew Bibles, but if not, prepare OHPs of the relevant passages.

Beginning

The Easter Greeting ('Christ is risen!' with the response 'He is risen indeed!') is still appropriate and can be used with the additional phrase 'And now he has ascended to the Father' with the response 'Come Holy Spirit!' Remind people that Ascension Day is the day when we remember that Jesus returned to heaven with a challenge and promises that we shall hear about later. If this service is being held on the Sunday after Ascension, then it is important to tell people that Ascension Day was actually the previous Thursday!

Songs

There are not many songs about Ascension Day, but many that involved the kingship of Jesus, such as 'Jesus is King', 'Jesus is the name we honour', 'He is exalted', 'Jesus shall take the highest honour' and the round 'King of kings and Lord of lords'. A modern hymn which can be used to begin the service could be 'Come, let us worship Jesus (King of the nations)' or the song 'Come, now is the time to worship' and 'Christ triumphant ever reigning' or 'Crown him with many crowns' would be a suitably glorious way to end the service.

Short talk

Put up an acetate with the words 'What's missing?' and see how many people notice the item which has been moved. When people do notice, deny that it is gone. When people insist that it has gone, say that it is actually still here. Eventually admit that people cannot see it – but that it is still in the building and you promise people will see it again.

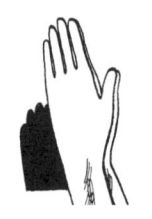

Prayer of Repentance

Either the Kyrie Confession for 'Word' on page 134 of *Common Worship*, or the 'Resurrection' Confession on page 125 may be appropriate.

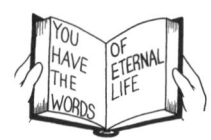

Bible reading

Read Acts 1:1-11 using a modern translation. This could be made visual by having a variety of people involved: a narrator, Jesus, a disciple and an angel with speaking parts, together with several other disciples and another angel with non-speaking parts. Rather than trying to create the illusion of Jesus 'disappearing', this could be achieved by asking the actor playing Jesus to walk up into the pulpit (and not standing up when they get inside) or create a diversion, such as shine a bright light into the roof of the church and encourage the disciples to look up to – thus diverting attention from the departing 'Jesus'!

Teaching

Encourage people to have a Bible to hand and turn to Acts 1 – get someone to shout out the page number (even if you know it, it encourages participation!). Say that Ascension day is all about (OHP 1) promises and a challenge.

Pick out the important aspects of the story in Acts 1 (OHP 2):
- Verse 3 – Jesus had proved to the disciples that he had risen from the dead.
- Verse 4 – Jesus promised the gift of the Holy Spirit.
- Verse 8 – Jesus told the disciples they had a job to do.
- Verse 9 – Jesus went back to heaven.
- Verse 10 – Angels told the disciples Jesus would return.

Ask why it was important that Jesus did go back to heaven.
Because if Jesus had not gone back to heaven:
- The Holy Spirit would not have come (John 16:7)
- Jesus needed to be reunited with his Father (John 14:20)

- The disciples would have relied on Jesus to do the job (Acts 1:8), but he wanted them to do the job.
- It would be easy for everyone in the world to be a Christian because Jesus would still be on earth, alive and well, and living in Israel! God wants people to have faith in Jesus *without* actually being able to see him.

So Ascension Day is important – say that Matthew also wrote about Ascension Day in Matthew 28:19-20 (OHP 3) and point out the challenge of Ascension Day and the promises of Ascension day (underlined on the OHP). Say that the challenge is still the same for us – to go and tell people about Jesus and encourage them to follow him, too. We might not be able to see Jesus (like the item in church) but we know that he *is* there and that the Holy Spirit helps us to know him better. The promises of Ascension Day are there, too, that he will be with us as we do it and he has sent the Holy Spirit to help us to do the job of telling people about him.

Statement of what we believe

The Affirmation on page 147 of *Common Worship* which is based on the Philippians 2 passage is suitable for Ascension day.

Intercessions and Lord's Prayer

In the 10 days between Ascension Day and Pentecost, Acts 1 tell us that the disciples constantly met together to pray and we believe that they were praising God for the fact that Jesus was now in his rightful place, in heaven with God his Father, and they prayed that Jesus' promise of the Holy Spirit would be fulfilled. Pray along the same lines, praying that Jesus would be King over all of our lives and that God would send the Holy Spirit to help us to fulfil Jesus' command to 'Go and make disciples'.

Ending

Remind people of the item which was removed before the service and that you have said although it cannot be seen, you know it is still in church. Say that when they come to church next time, you promise it will be back in place. Remind people that Jesus promised to return one day and that we should be looking out for him to do as he promised.

Ascension Day
is all about
Promises
and a
Challenge

OHP 2

- Verse 3: Jesus proved he was alive
- Verse 4: Jesus promised the Holy Spirit
- Verse 8: The disciples had a job
- Verse 9: Jesus went to heaven
- Verse 10: Jesus would return

Matthew's Story . . .

Therefore <u>go and make disciples</u> of all nations, <u>baptising them</u> in the name of the Father and of the Son and of the Holy Spirit, and <u>teaching them</u> to obey everything I have commanded you. And surely <u>I am with you always</u>, to the very end of the age.
Matthew 28:19-20

Luke's Story . . .

Do not leave Jerusalem, but <u>wait for the gift my Father promised</u>, which you have heard me speak about. For John baptised with water, but in a few days <u>you will be baptised with the Holy Spirit</u>.
Acts 1:4-5

Pentecost Sunday
Fruit, loverly fruit! (Acts 2:1-21)

- **What is the one thing you want them to take away?**
✓ The Fruit of the Spirit takes time to grow.
- **What is the one issue you want to challenge them about?**
✓ What Fruit is growing in your life?
- **What is the one thing you want them to apply in their lives?**
✓ To make sure it is being nurtured towards maturity.

The two main aspects of the work of the Holy Spirit are the Fruit of the Spirit and the Gifts of the Spirit. The Gifts are harder to explain, although children may not find the concept that difficult to grasp – the Fruit is a concept that is easier to convey and a vital one for adults and children alike to grasp!

Preparing the church

The main aim of the service is to show that plants take a long time to grow and the same is true of the Fruit of the Spirit. A bowl, laden with fruit, is the best and most important visual aid but anything involved in gardening or horticulture can be used as an aid: tools (the bigger and weirder the better!), seeds, plant pots, seedlings, fertiliser, watering cans . . . the list is endless! If you have access to a time-delayed video of a plant growing, it can be fascinating for the congregation to watch before the service begins (you might be able to get a copy from a school). Alternatively, a PowerPoint presentation of flowers or plants in various stages of growth could be effective. Or simply an acetate with a drawing of a tree laden with fruit. The simple message is 'growing fruit'!

Beginning

Many churches have a slot in their services to celebrate birthdays – even if you don't normally do so, ask if anyone has a birthday today. Find the person whose birthday is closest to today and wish them a happy birthday (possibly singing the 'Christian' words: *'Happy birthday to you/to Jesus be true/God bless you and keep you/happy birthday to you'*. Comment that Pentecost is the birthday of the Church because it was on the day of Pentecost that the church began, and also how much the church has grown from the few dozen people that followed Jesus at the start of the first day of Pentecost.

Songs

One thing is for sure at Pentecost – there are plenty of lively songs around! 'Jesus put this song into our hearts', 'In every circumstance of life' and 'Down the mountain the river flows (The river is here)' are appropriate and 'Give me oil in my lamp (Sing hosanna)' is well known in schools. There are plenty of more thoughtful songs, including 'Be still, for the presence of the Lord' and 'Holy Spirit, we welcome you'. 'Breathe on me, breath of God' is a good traditional hymn with which to finish.

Short talk

Take the bowl of fruit and ask people to name as many different fruits as they can – including the most obscure ones they can think of! Take a fruit from the bowl and ask about how it came to be like that and what it needed – teasing out the life-story of the fruit: a seed sown in the ground, watered, nurtured with the right amount of sun, water, nutrients, etc. Talk about the time it took for the plant to grow and the need for pruning and continued attention from the gardener, referring to the tools around you, etc. (OHP 1). Talk about the tree/plant and the way the fruit gradually appeared on it. Say that at Pentecost God gave the Holy Spirit to the church to fulfil the promise Jesus made and one effect of the Holy Spirit is what we call the Fruit of the Spirit, when the Holy Spirit helps us to be more like Jesus – and we'll find out more about it in a moment.

Prayer of Repentance

Introduce the Confession by saying that we all know that we do things which are not what Jesus would want us to do – use the Confession for 'City, World and Society' on page 127 of *Common Worship* with the fourth Absolution on page 135.

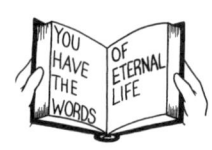

Bible reading

Read Acts 2:1-21 from a modern translation – the best version for this reading is probably *The Message*. Make sure whoever reads has practised the list of places – or get a prepared group of people (or people spread around the congregation) to shout out one of them as the list is read.

Teaching

Remind people of what we have said so far: that fruit takes a long time to grow and needs a lot of care for it to happen. If Bibles are available, turn to Galatians 5 and ask people to shout out the Fruit of the Spirit that are mentioned there. When they have been listed, put up the OHP with them all on (OHP 2).

Explain that when we look at Jesus we can see all of these fruit in him because he was full of the Holy Spirit. Jesus promised his friends before he died that he would send the Holy Spirit after he had gone back to heaven so that they would be able to live like he had done. On the Day of Pentecost the Holy Spirit came on his friends and every time someone becomes a Christian, and asks Jesus to be at the centre of their life, they receive the Holy Spirit, too. As they read their Bibles and talk to God, the Bible talks of them 'growing up' as Christians, as the Holy Spirit helps them to be more like Jesus, until, like the plants we talked about earlier, they start to produce fruit – the Fruit of the Spirit (OHP 3).

Whilst we know that there were people who did not like Jesus – there were lots and lots of people who did like Jesus. Why? We don't know what he looked like but there is nothing in the Bible that makes us think he looked any different from anyone else. It was because he was such a wonderful person to be around – because he was loving and joyful and had a deep peace within him, etc. So as we grow up as Christians and start to produce this fruit – so people will notice Jesus in us.

But it takes a long time – so don't worry, just keep doing all the things that will help us grow the Fruit of the Spirit.

Statement of what we believe

The creed based on Ephesians 3, number 7 on page 148 of *Common Worship*, is suitable.

Intercessions and Lord's Prayer

Going down the list of fruit in Galatians 5:22-23, apply each one to society or the community in which you live, asking for love in loveless places, peace in war-torn places, patience in places where the desire to achieve is overwhelming, etc.

Ending

Ask God to help all of us grow as Christians so that the Fruit will grow and other people will be attracted to Jesus.

The life-story of a fruit . . .

A seed sown in the ground,
watered, nurtured

It needs . . .
the right amount of sun, water, nutrients,
pruning and attention from the gardener

The Fruit of the Spirit is
love, joy, peace, patience,
kindness, goodness, faithfulness,
gentleness and self-control.

Galatians 5:22-23

The growth of a Christian . . .

Prayer

Reading the Bible

Coming to Church

and then . . .

. . . fruit will grow!

Trinity Sunday
Three into One WILL go (John 3:1-17)

- **What is the one thing you want them to take away?**
- ✓ The Trinity is an exciting mystery.
- **What is the one issue you want to challenge them about?**
- ✓ Are we willing to live with a faith that involves things we cannot understand?
- **What is the one thing you want them to apply in their lives?**
- ✓ That each member of the Trinity has an effect upon our lives.

Many people do not realise that although most Christians understand the concept of the Trinity, it is never actually mentioned as such in the Bible (although Jesus made a clear reference to it in Matthew 28:19). Most of us simply accept the Trinity without grappling with the implications. For children, the ability to think conceptually means that the Trinity is quite an exciting idea to think about. For adults it is more of a challenge! Issues relating to the male gender bias of the Trinity are sometimes raised in services concerning the Trinity – some of these issues are addressed in the service for Mother's Day.

Preparing the church

The Trinitarian symbol (see OHP 2) is one useful illustration of the Trinity – photocopy it on to an acetate and display it at the start of the service. Another way of trying to understand the Trinity is to find someone in the congregation who has a different role for different people. For example, I am '*my husband*, Tim' to my wife, I am '*Dad*' to my children and I am '*the Vicar*' to those in my congregation. Find someone who has three separate roles (e.g. a teacher, policeman, etc.) and ensure that they and the people with different perspectives are able to be at the service.

Beginning

Turn and greet each other with a Trinitarian handshake – 'I greet you in the name of the Father *(shake once in a normal fashion but don't let go)*, the Son *(twist your hands so that your thumb is vertical whilst grasping the other person's hand)* and the Holy Spirit *(maintaining the thumb grip, wave your fingers at each other)*. It is not as difficult as it sounds – but it is well worth practising with a friend in advance!

Songs

There are not many modern songs which grapple with the subject of the Trinity but 'Blessed be the name of the Lord', 'Lord, I come to you' and the quieter 'Faithful One' and 'Holy, Holy, Holy is the Lord' have a Trinitarian sense to them. The traditional hymn 'Holy, holy, Lord God Almighty' may be a glorious way to end the service.

Short talk

Ask whether anyone knows how a power station works. If you can find a picture, use an acetate with a diagram of a power station (as complicated as possible!) and explain that it is a very complex process. Ask who has switched on a light today. Note that we undertake a very simple action like switching on a light without any thought about the complicated process which has taken place in order for the light to work (OHP 1). We have faith (without even thinking about it) in the power companies that when we turn on a switch a light will come on, even though few (if any) of us have any understanding how it works.

Prayer of Repentance

The Confession on page 125 of *Common Worship* that is designated for Trinity is probably too wordy for All-age Worship whereas the General one on 128 may be more appropriate. The second Absolution on page 136 is suitable.

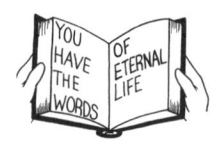

Bible reading

John 3:1-17 using a modern translation. The passage can be easily split into three voices: Narrator, Jesus and Nicodemus.

Teaching

Remind people of the talk earlier that often in life we have faith in things that we don't understand – and the same is true in our Christian faith. In the passage you have just read, God is mentioned in three ways: as God the Father (verses 16-17), God the Son (verses 14-16) and God the Spirit (verses 5-8). Throughout the Bible, we hear that there is one God and yet he is Father, Son and Holy Spirit – something that is really hard to understand.

Ask the person you have prepared to come forward and ask the congregation who this is. After people have named them, the other prepared individuals will disagree and offer their perspective on the person. Ask which is the right one – and get the answer (hopefully!) 'All of them'. Explain that the Trinity is a way of understanding that God has different sides to him, but there is only one God.

Show the Trinitarian symbol (OHP 2) and explain that this is a symbol that people have used for hundreds of years to help understand the Trinity. Has it one leaf or three? It is one symbol but with three clearly separate parts to it that helps us to understand (OHP 3). Go back to the passage and see the jobs mentioned of each member of the Trinity:

- Verse 16 – the Father sends the Son (Jesus).
- Verse 17 – the Son is sent to save the world.
- Verse 5 – the Spirit enables people to enter the kingdom of heaven.

It is hard to understand the Trinity – people have spent hundreds of years trying to explain it and have failed! The Bible tells us that God is wonderful – far more wonderful than we can possibly imagine and this means that we have to accept that there are some things that we will not be able to understand about God, but just trust that this is the way our wonderful God is!

Statement of what we believe

The Creed on page 144 of *Common Worship* is a simple way of stating a belief in a God who is Father, Son and Holy Spirit – but explain that the 'faith of the Church' is not about being able to understand the Trinity but accepting the Trinitarian God as a mystery.

Intercessions and Lord's Prayer

Include prayers that involve the different aspects of the Trinity: thanking God the Father for his parental care for us, asking that people in the world around us would accept Jesus for what he has done for the world and that the Holy Spirit would strengthen all of us in the task.

Ending

Repeat the Trinitarian handshake but this time as a blessing – 'God bless you in the name of the Father *(shake once in a normal fashion but don't let go)*, the Son *(twist your hands so that your thumb is vertical whilst grasping the other person's hand)* and the Holy Spirit *(maintaining the thumb grip, wave your fingers at each other)*. This time it should go better!

Faith in a light switch . . . simple!

Power Station

:

Wires

:

Our House

OHP 2

John 3
Verse 16 - the Father **sends**
Verse 17 - the Son is **sent**
Verse 5 - the Spirit **enables**

Harvest Sunday

Looking after God's world (Genesis 1:1-13)

(Not CW Lectionary Readings)

- **What is the one thing you want them to take away?**
✓ That in saying 'thank you' to God for the harvest produce, we also have to accept a responsibility for caring for God's world.

- **What is the one issue you want to challenge them about?**
✓ How much do we take care of the world around us?

- **What is the one thing you want them to apply in their lives?**
✓ An awareness that a small change in lifestyle can have a big effect when multiplied by millions of people.

Harvest is still a festival when visitors will come to church and the message of taking care of God's world is one that reaches far into the community. An understanding that we have been given responsibility rather than it being 'our' world is a subtle but important difference in the message.

Preparing the church

The church is likely to be 'dressed' traditionally, but it would be useful to have pictures of the world that display the beauty and variety of God's Creation. A table (for use in the opening talk) would be useful as would a set of children's building bricks (not the interlocking type such as Lego). A child primed as a 'helper' would be useful, too!

Beginning

A welcome that includes a reminder that we have come to thank God – because it is God who makes the produce grow and the farming community can do nothing without God's help!

Songs

The traditional Harvest hymns such as 'Come, ye thankful people, come' or 'We plough the fields and scatter ' are always appropriate ones to start and finish with (especially as the opening hymn involves the bringing forward of produce) but other songs such as 'Give thanks', 'Who paints the skies?' and 'God is good' are also applicable. If small children are present, 'God is good to me' may be fun to use!

Short talk

Ask for a helper and tell people that you want to build a tower with your building bricks. Build the tower as high (and therefore fragile) as possible – encouraging audience encouragement! Your helper will be primed to watch and then 'tinker' with the finished tower until it falls. Once you have finished your tower, talk about how proud you are of your creation and that you want your helper to keep an eye on it while you talk to the congregation. Amid (hopefully) cries of 'behind you!', the helper will tinker – when you turn round to check, they will promise not to damage it but to take careful charge of it. As you continue to talk about how long you hope the tower will last and that you know you can trust your helper, eventually the tinkering will lead to the fall of the tower. Ask the congregation how they think you must feel about what has happened ('angry', 'sad', 'frustrated', etc.) and comment that this is how God must feel with the way we have treated his creation.

Prayer of Repentance

There is a Harvest Confession on page 126 of *Common Worship* and the second Absolution on page 135 is appropriate.

Bible reading

Genesis 1:1-13 could be read using a modern translation and split up into different voices around the church. Be creative – perhaps using God's 'voice' with a microphone out of sight of the congregation.

Sketch/Poem

There are a few sketches and poems about Creation, such as 'The Other Story of the Garden of Eden', below, taken from *Conversations on the Way* (Tim Storey, Kevin Mayhew), which talk of God's sadness at Adam and Eve's failure to look after the Garden of Eden. This could be accompanied by either slides or a PowerPoint presentation illustrating the beauty of God's world contrasted with industrial pollution.

The Other Story of the Garden of Eden

And behold, the Lord God looked at his creation
and it was very good.

He looked at the sun and the moon and the stars,
he looked at the seas and the fish,
he looked at the mountains and the valleys,
he looked at the vast array of creatures, small and large,
he looked at the plants and the vegetation,
and, behold, it was very good.

And as the Lord God walked in the beautiful garden
he looked at the man he had made,
and he looked at the woman he had made
and thought, 'How long will it take you to mess all of this up?'

And so the Lord God spoke to the man and the woman and said,
'Because you two cannot be trusted –

if I turn my back for a minute
you'll be eating the apples that you shouldn't
and, before long, you will be cutting down trees
and killing animals that you don't need to
and will have turned this place of perfection
into a wasteland.

Because of all this
I am going to install a set of security cameras.
I am going to arrange for hourly patrols of angels
and I am going to insist that you do not take any decision
without it being in writing
and left with my personal secretary forty-eight hours before it is acted on.
I made this place perfect – and I want it to stay that way.'

And so the Lord God left the man and the woman in the garden
where, for an eternity, they lived happily
without any cares or responsibilities
and without any ability or desire to choose between right and wrong.

And somewhere in heaven
the book that was to be written
containing the stories of people
such as Cain and Abel, Moses, Elijah, David, Isaiah
and a host of others –
remained unwritten,
and the wondrous story of their failures
and their discoveries of God's love for them
was never heard
for it could never happen.

And the need, too, for God to send his only Son
to put the situation straight
well, that was never required.

The Lord God knew the man and the woman
he had created could not be trusted
with the precious gift they had been given,

and so his creation became a cold empty toy

and somehow it wasn't good any more.

Teaching

Taking the whole of Genesis 1, go through each of the things we are told that God created and ask the congregation to give examples of them (e.g. names of the planets, beautiful birds, glorious plants, etc.) and finish each section with the refrain 'and

God saw that it was ... GOOD', encouraging the children to join in as enthusiastically as possible. Using some of the produce that has been given, carry on the idea, inviting the congregation to say that the natural products we enjoy have been given to us by God and are 'GOOD!'.

Refer back to the earlier talk and also the sketch/poem – that it is very easy for people to mess up God's Creation and that is often what happens and it is up to us to make sure we take care of God's world. Invite suggestions as to how we might do this (e.g. recycling, turning lights off and not running water, thereby saving resources) and say that we want to leave God's world as we find it and that is 'GOOD!'.

Statement of what we believe

The Affirmation of Faith on page 144 of *Common Worship* talks of the Trinity as the source of life and is appropriate.

Intercessions and Lord's Prayer

Include prayers that acknowledge our failure to look after God's world and ask him to help us to be responsible for the resources we have been given.

Ending

Put up an acetate or piece of paper with the words 'God saw that it was GOOD – help us to keep it that way' and use a prayer that sums up the thoughts of the service.